TALKS

BY 'ABDU'L-BAHÁ

TALKS

BY 'ABDU'L-BAHÁ

THE

ETERNAL

COVENANT

Bahá'í
PUBLISHING
Wilmette, Illinois

Bahá'í Publishing
415 Linden Avenue, Wilmette, Illinois 60091-2844
Copyright © 2011 by the National Spiritual Assembly of
the Bahá'ís of the United States

All rights reserved. Published 2011
Printed in the United States of America on acid-free paper ∞

14   13   12   4   3   2

Library of Congress Cataloging-in-Publication Data

'Abdu'l-Bahá, 1844–1921.
  [Speeches. English. Selections.]
  Talks by 'Abdu'l-Bahá : the eternal covenant / 'Abdu'l-Bahá.
      p. cm.
  A collection of talks given by 'Abdu'l-Bahá during his journey to North
America in 1912.
  Includes bibliographical references.
  ISBN 978-1-931847-82-7 (alk. paper)
  1. Spirituality. 2. Bahai Faith—Doctrines. I. Title.
  BP363.A3 2011
  297.9'34—dc22
                                                        2011000199

Cover design by Andrew Johnson
Book design by Patrick Falso

Religions are many, but the reality of religion is one.
The days are many, but the sun is one.
The fountains are many, but the fountainhead is one.
The branches are many, but the tree is one.

—'Abdu'l-Bahá

Introduction

In 1912, a man known as 'Abdu'l-Bahá arrived on the shores of North America. He was sixty-seven years of age and had spent the majority of his life as a prisoner of the Ottoman Empire. At the time of his visit, he was the head of a little-known religious community called the Bahá'í Faith. Few people in the Western world knew of the Faith he represented and fewer still had ever heard his name. 'Abdu'l-Bahá's extraordinary visit to these shores had such a monumental impact on all those with whom he came in contact, however, that history continues to shed light on its significance

The Bahá'í Faith, the newest of the independent world religions, was founded in 1844 in what is now Iran and owes its origin to the labors of two successive founding Prophets: the Báb and Bahá'u'lláh. As the Báb explained, His mission was to prepare the way for "Him Whom God shall make manifest," the Manifestation of God awaited by the followers of all faiths. During the course of successive waves of persecution that followed this announcement and that claimed the lives of the Báb and several thousands of His followers, Bahá'u'lláh declared Himself to be the fulfillment of the divine promise.

Introduction

'Abdu'l-Bahá (23 May 1844–28 November 1921) was the eldest surviving son and designated successor to Bahá'u'lláh, the Prophet-Founder of the Bahá'í Faith. Though he was known as "'Abbas Effendi" outside of the Bahá'í community, Bahá'ís often refer to him as "the Most Great Branch," "the Mystery of God," and "the Master"—titles bestowed on him by Bahá'u'lláh. After Bahá'u'lláh's passing in 1892, he chose to refer to himself as "'Abdu'l-Bahá," meaning "Servant of the Glory."

From the age of eight, 'Abdu'l-Bahá shared the exile and imprisonment of his father at the hands of the Ottoman Empire. Two years after finally being freed from prison at the age of sixty-seven, undeterred by poor health that was the result of a lifetime of hardship and suffering, he set out from Palestine (present-day Israel) on a momentous series of journeys throughout Europe and the United States. His purpose was to share the teachings and vision of Bahá'u'lláh with the people of the West. Over the course of his journeys, 'Abdu'l-Bahá gave a series of public addresses, which have been documented in a number of books. Speaking in Persian with the aid of a translator, he shared profound insights on a number of topics in a simple manner, accessible to anyone who listened with an open heart. 'Abdu'l-Bahá spoke on matters of spirituality as well as on the condition of the world. He shed light on complex matters of the soul and the spiritual nature of man, while addressing issues concerning society at large.

Collected in this volume is a series of talks by 'Abdu'l-Bahá that deal with subjects related to the eternal covenant of God—a theme that is central to the Bahá'í teachings. According to this eternal covenant, God never leaves humankind without guidance, but rather makes His will and purpose known to us through the appearance of His Prophets or Manifestations, Who appear periodically throughout history to advance human civilization. From a Bahá'í perspective, there is only one true God and one true religion, which gradually unfolds over time. *The Eternal Covenant* contains talks by 'Abdu'l-Bahá that touch on this theme as well as addressing various other issues of vital importance. These talks have helped many gain a clearer understanding of otherwise complex topics, and it is hoped that readers of all faiths will gain valuable insights from this collection.

5 May 1912

TALK AT PLYMOUTH CONGREGATIONAL CHURCH

---

935 East Fiftieth Street
Chicago, Illinois

Notes by Marzieh Moss

I offer thanks to God for the privilege of being present in an assemblage which is commemorating Him, whose members have no thought or intention save His good pleasure and the unbiased investigation of reality. I praise God for this meeting of human souls free from the bondage of imitations and prejudice, willing to examine reasonably and accept that which is found to be true.

In our solar system the center of illumination is the sun itself. Through the will of God this central luminary is the one source of the existence and development of all phenomenal things. When we observe the organisms of the material kingdoms, we find that their growth and training are dependent upon the heat and light of the sun. Without this quickening impulse there would be no growth of tree or vegetation; neither would the existence of animal or human being be possible; in fact, no forms of created life would be manifest upon the earth. But if we reflect deeply, we will perceive that the great bestower and giver of life is God; the sun is the intermediary of His will and plan. Without the bounty of the sun, therefore, the world would be in darkness. All illumination of our planetary system proceeds or emanates from the solar center.

Likewise, in the spiritual realm of intelligence and idealism there must be a center of illumination, and that center is the everlasting, ever-shining Sun, the Word of God. Its lights are the lights of reality which have shone upon humanity, illumining the realm of thought and morals, conferring the bounties of the divine world upon man. These lights are the cause of the education of souls and the source of the enlightenment of hearts, sending forth in effulgent radiance the message of the glad tidings of the kingdom of God. In brief, the moral and ethical world and the world of spiritual regeneration are dependent for their progressive being upon that heavenly Center of illumination. It gives forth the light of religion and bestows the life of the spirit, imbues humanity with archetypal virtues and confers eternal splendors. This Sun of Reality, this Center of effulgences, is the Prophet or Manifestation of God. Just as the phenomenal sun shines upon the material world producing life and growth, likewise, the spiritual or prophetic Sun confers illumination upon the human world of thought and intelligence, and unless it rose upon the horizon of human existence, the kingdom of man would become dark and extinguished.

The Sun of Reality is one Sun, but it has different dawning places, just as the phenomenal sun is one although it appears at various points of the horizon. During the time of summer the luminary of the physical world rises far to the north of the equinoctial, in spring and fall it dawns midway, and in winter it appears in the most southerly point of its zodiacal journey. These daysprings or dawning points differ widely, but the sun is ever the same sun—whether it be the phenomenal or spiritual luminary. Souls who focus their vision upon the Sun of Reality will be the recipients of light no matter from what point it rises, but those who are fettered by adoration of the dawning point are deprived when it appears in a different station upon the spiritual horizon.

Furthermore, just as the solar cycle has its four seasons, the cycle of the Sun of Reality has its distinct and successive periods. Each brings its vernal season or springtime. When the Sun of Reality returns to quicken the world of mankind, a divine bounty descends from the heaven of generosity. The realm of thoughts and ideals is set in motion and blessed with new life. Minds are developed, hopes brighten, aspirations become spiritual, the virtues of the human world appear with freshened power of growth, and the image and likeness of God become visible in man. It is the springtime of the inner world. After the spring, summer comes with its fullness and spiritual fruitage; autumn follows with its withering winds which chill the soul; the Sun seems to be going away, until at last the mantle of winter overspreads, and only faint traces of the effulgence of that divine Sun remain. Just as the surface of the material world becomes dark and dreary, the soil dormant, the trees naked and bare and no beauty or freshness remains to cheer the darkness and desolation, so the winter of the spiritual cycle witnesses the death and disappearance of divine growth and extinction of the light and love of God. But again the cycle begins and a new springtime appears. In it the former springtime has returned; the world is resuscitated, illumined and attains spirituality; religion is renewed and reorganized, hearts are turned to God, the summons of God is heard, and life is again bestowed upon man. For a long time the religious world had been weakened and materialism had advanced; the spiritual forces of life were waning, moralities were becoming degraded, composure and peace had vanished from souls, and satanic qualities were dominating hearts; strife and hatred overshadowed humanity, bloodshed and violence prevailed. God was neglected; the Sun of Reality seemed to have gone completely; deprivation of the bounties of heaven was a fact; and so the season of winter fell upon mankind. But in the generosity of God a new springtime dawned, the lights of God shone forth, the effulgent Sun of Reality returned and became manifest, the realm of thoughts and kingdom of hearts became exhilarated, a new spirit of life breathed into the body of the world, and continuous advancement became apparent.

I hope that the lights of the Sun of Reality will illumine the whole world so that no strife and warfare, no battles and bloodshed remain. May fanaticism and religious bigotry be unknown, all humanity enter the bond of brotherhood, souls consort in perfect agreement, the nations of earth at last hoist the banner of truth, and the religions of the world enter the divine temple of oneness, for the foundations of the heavenly religions are one reality. Reality is not divisible; it does not admit multiplicity. All the holy Manifestations of God have proclaimed and promulgated the same reality. They have summoned mankind to reality itself, and reality is one. The clouds and mists of imitations have obscured the Sun of Truth. We must forsake these imitations, dispel these clouds and mists and free the Sun from the darkness of superstition. Then will the Sun of Truth shine most gloriously; then all the inhabitants of the world will be united, the religions will be one, sects and denominations will reconcile, all nationalities will flow together in the recognition of one Fatherhood, and all degrees of humankind will gather in the shelter of the same tabernacle, under the same banner.

Until the heavenly civilization is founded, no result will be forthcoming from material civilization, even as you observe. See what catastrophes overwhelm mankind. Consider the wars which disturb the world. Consider the enmity and hatred. The existence of these wars and conditions indicates and proves that the heavenly civilization has not yet been established. If the civilization of the Kingdom be spread to all the nations, this dust of disagreement will be dispelled, these clouds will pass away, and the Sun of Reality in its greatest effulgence and glory will shine upon mankind.

O God! O Thou Who givest! This congregation is turning to Thee, casting their glances toward Thy Kingdom and favor, longing to behold the lights of Thy face. O God! Bless this nation. Confirm this government. Reveal Thy glory unto this people and confer upon them life eternal. O God! Illumine the faces, render the hearts radiant, exhilarate the breasts, crown the heads with the diadem of Thy providence, cause them to soar in Thy pure atmosphere so they may reach the highest pinnacles of Thy splendor. Assist them in order that this world may ever find the light and effulgence of Thy presence. O God! Shelter this congregation and admonish this nation. Render them progressive in all degrees. May they become leaders in the world of humanity. May they be Thine examples among humankind. May they be manifestations of Thy grace. May they be filled with the inspiration of Thy Word. Thou art the Powerful. Thou art the Mighty. Thou art the Giver, and Thou art the Omniscient.

5 MAY 1912

———————————

TALK AT
ALL-SOULS CHURCH

———————————

LINCOLN CENTER,
CHICAGO, ILLINOIS

Notes by Marzieh Moss

The divine religions were founded for the purpose of unifying humanity and establishing universal peace. Any movement which brings about peace and agreement in human society is truly a divine movement; any reform which causes people to come together under the shelter of the same tabernacle is surely animated by heavenly motives. At all times and in all ages of the world, religion has been a factor in cementing together the hearts of men and in uniting various and divergent creeds. It is the peace element in religion that blends mankind and makes for unity. Warfare has ever been the cause of separation, disunion and discord.

Consider how Jesus Christ united the divergent peoples, sects and denominations of the early days. It is evident that the fundamentals of religion are intended to unify and bind together; their purpose is universal, everlasting peace. Prior to the time of Jesus Christ the Word of God had unified opposite types and conflicting elements of human society; and since His appearance the divine Teachers of the primal principles of the law of God have all intended this universal outcome. In Persia Bahá'u'lláh was able to unite people of varying thought, creed and denomination. The inhabitants of that country were Christians, Muslims, Jews, Zoroastrians and a great variety of subdivided forms and beliefs together with racial distinctions such as Semitic, Arabic, Persian, Turk, etc.; but through the power and efficacy of religion Bahá'u'lláh united these differing peoples and caused them to consort together in perfect agreement. Such unity and accord became manifest among them that they were considered as one people and one kind.

The cause of this fellowship and unity lies in the fact that the divine law has two distinct aspects or functions: one the essential or fundamental, the other the material or accidental. The first aspect of the revealed religion of God is that which concerns the ethical development and spiritual progress of mankind, the awakening of potential human susceptibilities and the descent of divine bestowals. These ordinances are changeless, essential, eternal. The second function of the divine religion deals with material conditions, the laws of human intercourse and social regulation. These are subject to change and transformation in accordance with the time, place and conditions. The essential ordinances of religion were the same during the time of Abraham, the day of Moses and the cycle of Jesus, but the accidental or material laws were abrogated and superseded according to the exigency and requirement of each succeeding age. For example, in the law of Moses there were ten distinct commandments in regard to murder, which were revealed according to the requirement and capacity of the people, but in the day of Jesus these were abrogated and superseded in conformity with the changed and advanced human conditions.

The central purpose of the divine religions is the establishment of peace and unity among mankind. Their reality is one; therefore, their accomplishment is one and universal—whether it be through the essential or material ordinances of God. There is but one light of the material sun, one ocean, one rain, one atmosphere. Similarly, in the spiritual world there is one divine reality forming the center and altruistic basis for peace and reconciliation among various and conflicting nations and peoples. Consider how the Roman Empire and Greek nation were at war in enmity and hatred after the Messianic day, how the hostilities of Egypt and Assyria, though subdued in intensity, still flamed in the warring element of these ancient and declining nations. But the teachings of Jesus Christ proved to be the cement by which they were united; warfare ceased, strife and hatred passed away, and these belligerent peoples associated in love and friendship. For strife and warfare are the very destroyers of human foundations, whereas peace and amity are the builders and safeguards of human welfare. As an instance, two nations which have remained at peace for centuries declare war against each other. What destruction and loss befalls both in one year of strife and conflict—the undoing of centuries. How urgent their necessity and demand for peace, with its comfort and progress, instead of war, which blasts and destroys the foundation of all human attainment.

The body politic may be likened to the human organism. As long as the various members and parts of that organism are coordinated and cooperating in harmony, we have as a result the expression of life in its fullest degree. When these members lack coordination and harmony, we have the reverse, which in the human organism is disease, dissolution, death. Similarly, in the body politic of humanity dissension, discord and warfare are always destructive and inevitably fatal. All created beings are dependent upon peace and coordination, for every contingent and phenomenal being is a composition of distinct elements. As long as there is affinity and cohesion among these constituent elements, strength and life are manifest; but when dissension and repulsion arise among them, disintegration follows. This is proof that peace and amity, which God has willed for His children, are the saving factors of human society, whereas war and strife, which violate His ordinances, are the cause of death and destruction. Therefore, God has sent His Prophets to announce the message of goodwill, peace and life to the world of mankind.

Inasmuch as the essential reality of the religions is one and their seeming variance and plurality is adherence to forms and imitations which have arisen, it is evident that these causes of difference and divergence must be abandoned in order that the underlying reality may unite mankind in its enlightenment and up-building. All who hold fast to the one reality will be in agreement and unity. Then shall the religions summon people to the oneness of the world of humanity and to universal justice; then will they proclaim equality of rights and exhort men to virtue and to faith in the loving mercy of God. The underlying foundation of the religions is one; there is no intrinsic difference between them. Therefore, if the essential and fundamental ordinances of the religions be observed, peace and unity will dawn, and all the differences of sects and denominations will disappear.

And now let us consider the various peoples of the world. All the nations—American, British, French, German, Turkish, Persian, Arab—are children of the same Adam, members of the same human household. Why should dissension exist among them? The surface of the earth is one native land, and that native land was provided for all. God has not set these boundaries and race limitations. Why should imaginary barriers which God has not originally destined be made a cause of contention? God has created and provided for all. He is the Preserver of all, and all are submerged in the ocean of His mercy. Not a single soul is deprived. Inasmuch as we have such a loving God and Creator, why should we be at war with each other? Now that His light is shining universally, why should we cast ourselves into darkness? As His table is spread for all His children, why should we deprive each other of its sustenance? As His effulgence is shining upon all, why should we seek to live among the shadows? There is no doubt that the only cause is ignorance and that the result is perdition. Discord deprives humanity of the eternal favors of God; therefore, we must forget all imaginary causes of difference and seek the very fundamentals of the divine religions in order that we may associate in perfect love and accord and consider humankind as one family, the surface of the earth as one nationality and all races as one humanity. Let us live under the protection of God, attaining eternal happiness in this world and everlasting life in the world to come.

O Thou kind Lord! Thou hast created all humanity from the same stock. Thou hast decreed that all shall belong to the same household. In Thy Holy Presence they are all Thy servants, and all mankind are sheltered beneath Thy Tabernacle; all have gathered together at Thy Table of Bounty; all are illumined through the light of Thy Providence.

O God! Thou art kind to all, Thou hast provided for all, dost shelter all, conferrest life upon all. Thou hast endowed each and all with talents and faculties, and all are submerged in the Ocean of Thy Mercy.

O Thou kind Lord! Unite all. Let the religions agree and make the nations one, so that they may see each other as one family and the whole earth as one home. May they all live together in perfect harmony.

O God! Raise aloft the banner of the oneness of mankind.

O God! Establish the Most Great Peace.

Cement Thou, O God, the hearts together.

O Thou kind Father, God! Gladden our hearts through the fragrance of Thy love. Brighten our eyes through the Light of Thy Guidance. Delight our ears with the melody of Thy Word, and shelter us all in the Stronghold of Thy Providence.

Thou art the Mighty and Powerful, Thou art the Forgiving and Thou art the One Who overlooketh the shortcomings of all mankind.

7 May 1912

TALK AT
HOTEL SCHENLEY

Pittsburgh, Pennsylvania

Notes by Suza

I have come from the Orient to visit your country. Surely this continent is praiseworthy from all points of view, and there are signs of prosperity everywhere. The people show refinement, and evidences of progressive civilization abound. I will give you a brief exposition of the fundamental principles of Bahá'u'lláh's teachings in order that you may be informed of the nature and significance of the Bahá'í movement.

About sixty years ago the greatest enmity and strife existed among the various peoples and religious denominations of Persia. Throughout the world generally war and dissension prevailed. At this time Bahá'u'lláh appeared in Persia and began devoting Himself to the uplift and education of the people. He united divergent sects and creeds, removed religious, racial, patriotic and political prejudices and established a strong bond of unity and reconciliation among varying degrees and classes of mankind. The enmity then existing among the people was so bitter and intense that even ordinary association was out of the question. They would not meet and consult with each other at all. Through the power of the teachings of Bahá'u'lláh the most wonderful results were witnessed. He removed the prejudices and hatred from human hearts and wrought such transformation in their attitudes toward each other that today in Persia there is perfect accord among hitherto bigoted religionists, varying sects and divergent classes. This was not an easy accomplishment, for Bahá'u'lláh underwent severe trials, great difficulties and violent persecution. He was imprisoned, tortures were inflicted upon Him, and finally He was banished from His native land. He bore every ordeal and infliction cheerfully. In His successive exiles from country to country up to the time of His ascension from this world, He was enabled to promulgate His teachings, even from prison. Wherever His oppressors sent Him, He hoisted the standard of the oneness of the world of humanity and promulgated the principles of the unity of mankind. Some of these principles are as follows. First, it is incumbent upon all mankind to investigate truth. If such investigation be made, all should agree and be united, for truth or reality is not multiple; it is not divisible. The different religions have one truth underlying them; therefore, their reality is one.

Each of the divine religions embodies two kinds of ordinances. The first is those which concern spiritual susceptibilities, the development of moral principles and the quickening of the conscience of man. These are essential or fundamental, one and the same in all religions, changeless and eternal—reality not subject to transformation. Abraham heralded this reality, Moses promulgated it, and Jesus Christ established it in the world of mankind. All the divine Prophets and Messengers were the instruments and channels of this same eternal, essential truth.

The second kind of ordinances in the divine religions is those which relate to the material affairs of humankind. These are the material or accidental laws which are subject to change in each day of manifestation, according to exigencies of the time, conditions and differing capacities of humanity. For instance, in the day of Moses ten commandments in regard to murder were revealed by Him. These commandments were in accordance with the requirements of that day and time. Other laws embodying drastic punishments were enacted by Moses—an eye for an eye, a tooth for a tooth. The penalty for theft was amputation of the hand. These laws and penalties were applicable to the degree of the Israelitish people of that period, who dwelt in the wilderness and desert under conditions where severity was necessary and justifiable. But in the time of Jesus Christ this kind of law was not expedient; therefore, Christ abrogated and superseded the commands of Moses.

In brief, every one of the divine religions contains essential ordinances, which are not subject to change, and material ordinances, which are abrogated according to the exigencies of time. But the people of the world have forsaken the divine teachings and followed forms and imitations of the truth. Inasmuch as these human interpretations and superstitions differ, dissensions and bigotry have arisen, and strife and warfare have prevailed. By investigating the truth or foundation of reality underlying their own and other beliefs, all would be united and agreed, for this reality is one; it is not multiple and not divisible.

The second principle or teaching of Bahá'u'lláh is the proclamation of the oneness of the world of humanity—that all are servants of God and belong to one family; that God has created all and, therefore, His bestowals are universal; and that His providence, training, sustenance and loving-kindness surround all mankind.

This is the divine policy, and it is impossible for man to lay the foundation of a better plan and policy than that which God has instituted. Therefore, we must recognize and assist the purpose of the glorious Lord. Inasmuch as God is kind and loving to all, why should we be unkind? As this human world is one household, why should its members be occupied with animosity and contention? Therefore, humanity must be looked upon with the eye of equal estimate and in the same attitude of love. The noblest of men is he who serves humankind, and he is nearest the threshold of God who is the least of His servants. The glory and majesty of man are dependent upon his servitude to his fellow creatures and not upon the exercise of hostility and hatred.

The third principle or teaching of Bahá'u'lláh is the oneness of religion and science. Any religious belief which is not conformable with scientific proof and investigation is superstition, for true science is reason and reality, and religion is essentially reality and pure reason; therefore, the two must correspond. Religious teaching which is at variance with science and reason is human invention and imagination unworthy of acceptance, for the antithesis and opposite of knowledge is superstition born of the ignorance of man. If we say religion is opposed to science, we lack knowledge of either true science or true religion, for both are founded upon the premises and conclusions of reason, and both must bear its test.

The fourth principle or teaching of Bahá'u'lláh is the readjustment and equalization of the economic standards of mankind. This deals with the question of human livelihood. It is evident that under present systems and conditions of government the poor are subject to the greatest need and distress while others more fortunate live in luxury and plenty far beyond their actual necessities. This inequality of portion and privilege is one of the deep and vital problems of human society. That there is need of an equalization and apportionment by which all may possess the comforts and privileges of life is evident. The remedy must be legislative readjustment of conditions. The rich too must be merciful to the poor, contributing from willing hearts to their needs without being forced or compelled to do so. The composure of the world will be assured by the establishment of this principle in the religious life of mankind.

The fifth principle or teaching of Bahá'u'lláh is the abandoning of religious, racial, patriotic and political prejudices, which destroy the foundations of human society. All mankind are creatures and servants of the one God. The surface of the earth is one home; humanity is one family and household. Distinctions and boundaries are artificial, human. Why should there be discord and strife among men? All must become united and coordinated in service to the world of humanity.

The sixth principle or teaching of Bahá'u'lláh concerns the equality of man and woman. He has declared that in the estimation of God there is no distinction of sex. The one whose heart is most pure, whose deeds and service in the Cause of God are greater and nobler, is most acceptable before the divine threshold—whether male or female. In the vegetable and animal kingdoms sex exists in perfect equality and without distinction or invidious estimate. The animal, although inferior to man in intelligence and reason, recognizes sex equality. Why should man, who is endowed with the sense of justice and sensibilities of conscience, be willing that one of the members of the human family should be rated and considered as subordinate? Such differentiation is neither intelligent nor conscientious; therefore, the principle of religion has been revealed by Bahá'u'lláh that woman must be given the privilege of equal education with man and full right to his prerogatives. That is to say, there must be no difference in the education of male and female in order that womankind may develop equal capacity and importance with man in the social and economic equation. Then the world will attain unity and harmony. In past ages humanity has been defective and inefficient because it has been incomplete. War and its ravages have blighted the world; the education of woman will be a mighty step toward its abolition and ending, for she will use her whole influence against war. Woman rears the child and educates the youth to maturity. She will refuse to give her sons for sacrifice upon the field of battle. In truth, she will be the greatest factor in establishing universal peace and international arbitration. Assuredly, woman will abolish warfare among mankind. Inasmuch as human society consists of two parts, the male and female, each the complement of the other, the happiness and stability of humanity cannot be assured unless both are perfected. Therefore, the standard and status of man and woman must become equalized.

Among other teachings and principles Bahá'u'lláh counsels the education of all members of society. No individual should be denied or deprived of intellectual training, although each should receive according to capacity. None must be left in the grades of ignorance, for ignorance is a defect in the human world. All mankind must be given a knowledge of science and philosophy—that is, as much as may be deemed necessary. All cannot be scientists and philosophers, but each should be educated according to his needs and deserts.

Bahá'u'lláh teaches that the world of humanity is in need of the breath of the Holy Spirit, for in spiritual quickening and enlightenment true oneness is attained with God and man. The Most Great Peace cannot be assured through racial force and effort; it cannot be established by patriotic devotion and sacrifice; for nations differ widely and local patriotism has limitations. Furthermore, it is evident that political power and diplomatic ability are not conducive to universal agreement, for the interests of governments are varied and selfish; nor will international harmony and reconciliation be an outcome of human opinions concentrated upon it, for opinions are faulty and intrinsically diverse. Universal peace is an impossibility through human and material agencies; it must be through spiritual power. There is need of a universal impelling force which will establish the oneness of humanity and destroy the foundations of war and strife. None other than the divine power can do this; therefore, it will be accomplished through the breath of the Holy Spirit.

No matter how far the material world advances, it cannot establish the happiness of mankind. Only when material and spiritual civilization are linked and coordinated will happiness be assured. Then material civilization will not contribute its energies to the forces of evil in destroying the oneness of humanity, for in material civilization good and evil advance together and maintain the same pace. For example, consider the material progress of man in the last decade. Schools and colleges, hospitals, philanthropic institutions, scientific academies and temples of philosophy have been founded, but hand in hand with these evidences of development, the invention and production of means and weapons for human destruction have correspondingly increased. In early days the weapon of war was the sword; now it is the magazine rifle. Among the ancients, men fought with javelins and daggers; now they employ shells and bombs. Dreadnoughts are built, torpedoes invented, and every few days new ammunition is forthcoming.

All this is the outcome of material civilization; therefore, although material advancement furthers good purposes in life, at the same time it serves evil ends. The divine civilization is good because it cultivates morals. Consider what the Prophets of God have contributed to human morality. Jesus Christ summoned all to the Most Great Peace through the acquisition of pure morals. If the moral precepts and foundations of divine civilization become united with the material advancement of man, there is no doubt that the happiness of the human world will be attained and that from every direction the glad tidings of peace upon earth will be announced. Then humankind will achieve extraordinary progress, the sphere of human intelligence will be immeasurably enlarged, wonderful inventions will appear, and the spirit of God will reveal itself; all men will consort in joy and fragrance, and eternal life will be conferred upon the children of the Kingdom. Then will the power of the divine make itself effective and the breath of the Holy Spirit penetrate the essence of all things. Therefore, the material and the divine, or merciful, civilizations must progress together until the highest aspirations and desires of humanity shall become realized.

These are a few of the teachings and principles of Bahá'u'lláh, briefly presented so that you may be informed of their significance and purpose and find them a stimulus to your knowledge and actions. I ask God to assist this prosperous and progressive nation and to bestow His blessings upon this just government and wonderful continent of the West.

12 May 1912

———————————

TALK AT
UNITY CHURCH

———————————

Montclair, New Jersey

Notes by Esther Foster

I wish to speak upon the subject of divine unity, the oneness of God, before this revered assemblage.

It is a self-evident fact that phenomenal existence can never grasp nor comprehend the ancient and essential Reality. Utter weakness cannot understand absolute strength. When we view the world of creation, we discover differences in degree which make it impossible for the lower to comprehend the higher. For example, the mineral kingdom, no matter how much it may advance, can never comprehend the phenomena of the vegetable kingdom. Whatever development the vegetable may attain, it can have no message from nor come in touch with the kingdom of the animal. However perfect may be the growth of a tree, it cannot realize the sensation of sight, hearing, smell, taste and touch; these are beyond its limitation. Although it is the possessor of existence in the world of creation, a tree, nevertheless, has no knowledge of the superior degree of the animal kingdom. Likewise, no matter how great the advancement of the animal, it can have no idea of the human plane, no knowledge of intellect and spirit. Difference in degree is an obstacle to this comprehension. A lower degree cannot comprehend a higher although all are in the same world of creation—whether mineral, vegetable or animal.

Degree is the barrier and limitation. In the human plane of existence we can say we have knowledge of a vegetable, its qualities and product; but the vegetable has no knowledge or comprehension whatever of us. No matter how near perfection this rose may advance in its own sphere, it can never possess hearing and sight. Inasmuch as in the creational world, which is phenomenal, difference of degree is an obstacle or hindrance to comprehension, how can the human being, which is a created exigency, comprehend the ancient divine Reality, which is essential? This is impossible because the reality of Divinity is sanctified beyond the comprehension of the created being, man.

Furthermore, that which man can grasp is finite to man, and man to it is as infinite. Is it possible then for the reality of Divinity to be finite and the human creature infinite? On the contrary, the reverse is true; the human is finite while the essence of Divinity is infinite. Whatever comes within the sphere of human comprehension must be limited and finite. As the essence of Divinity transcends the comprehension of man, therefore God brings forth certain Manifestations of the divine Reality upon Whom He bestows heavenly effulgences in order that They may be intermediaries between humanity and Himself. These holy Manifestations or Prophets of God are as mirrors which have acquired illumination from the Sun of Truth, but the Sun does not descend from its high zenith and does not effect entrance within the mirror. In truth, this mirror has attained complete polish and purity until the utmost capacity of reflection has been developed in it; therefore, the Sun of Reality with its fullest effulgence and splendor is revealed therein. These mirrors are earthly, whereas the reality of Divinity is in its highest apogee. Although its lights are shining and its heat is manifest in them, although these mirrors are telling their story of its effulgence, the Sun, nevertheless, remains in its own lofty station; it does not descend; it does not effect entrance, because it is holy and sanctified.

The Sun of Divinity and of Reality has revealed itself in various mirrors. Though these mirrors are many, yet the Sun is one. The bestowals of God are one; the reality of the divine religion is one. Consider how one and the same light has reflected itself in the different mirrors or manifestations of it. There are certain souls who are lovers of the Sun; they perceive the effulgence of the Sun from every mirror. They are not fettered or attached to the mirrors; they are attached to the Sun itself and adore it, no matter from what point it may shine. But those who adore the mirror and are attached to it become deprived of witnessing the light of the Sun when it shines forth from another mirror. For instance, the Sun of Reality revealed itself from the Mosaic mirror. The people who were sincere accepted and believed in it. When the same Sun shone from the Messianic mirror, the Jews who were not lovers of the Sun and who were fettered by their adoration of the mirror of Moses did not perceive the lights and effulgences of the Sun of Reality resplendent in Jesus; therefore, they were deprived of its bestowals. Yet the Sun of Reality, the Word of God, shone from the Messianic mirror through the wonderful channel of Jesus Christ more fully and more wonderfully. Its effulgences were manifestly radiant, but even to this day the Jews are holding to the Mosaic mirror. Therefore, they are bereft of witnessing the lights of eternity in Jesus.

In brief, the sun is one sun, the light is one light which shines upon all phenomenal beings. Every creature has a portion thereof, but the pure mirror can reveal the story of its bounty more fully and completely. Therefore, we must adore the light of the Sun, no matter through what mirror it may be revealed. We must not entertain prejudice, for prejudice is an obstacle to realization. Inasmuch as the effulgence is one effulgence, the human realities must all become recipients of the same light, recognizing in it the compelling force that unites them in its illumination.

As this is the radiant century, it is my hope that the Sun of Truth may illumine all humanity. May the eyes be opened and the ears become attentive; may souls become resuscitated and consort together in the utmost harmony as recipients of the same light. Perchance, God will remove this strife and warfare of thousands of years. May this bloodshed pass away, this tyranny and oppression cease, this warfare be ended. May the light of love shine forth and illumine hearts, and may human lives be cemented and connected until all of us may find agreement and tranquillity beneath the same tabernacle and with the standard of the Most Great Peace above us move steadily onward.

O Thou kind Lord! O Thou Who art generous
and merciful! We are the servants of Thy threshold
and are gathered beneath the sheltering shadow of
Thy divine unity. The sun of Thy mercy is shining
upon all, and the clouds of Thy bounty shower upon
all. Thy gifts encompass all, Thy loving providence
sustains all, Thy protection overshadows all, and the
glances of Thy favor are cast upon all. O Lord! Grant
Thine infinite bestowals, and let the light of Thy
guidance shine. Illumine the eyes, gladden the hearts
with abiding joy. Confer a new spirit upon all people
and bestow upon them eternal life. Unlock the gates
of true understanding and let the light of faith shine
resplendent. Gather all people beneath the shadow of
Thy bounty and cause them to unite in harmony, so
that they may become as the rays of one sun, as the
waves of one ocean, and as the fruit of one tree. May
they drink from the same fountain. May they be refreshed by the same breeze. May they receive illumination from the same source of light. Thou art the
Giver, the Merciful, the Omnipotent.

19 May 1912

TALK AT CHURCH OF THE DIVINE PATERNITY

Central Park West,
New York

Notes by Esther Foster

R eligions are many, but the reality of religion is one. The days are many, but the sun is one. The fountains are many, but the fountainhead is one. The branches are many, but the tree is one.

The foundation of the divine religions is reality; were there no reality, there would be no religions. Abraham heralded reality. Moses promulgated reality. Christ established reality. Muḥammad was the Messenger of reality. The Báb was the door of reality. Bahá'u'lláh was the splendor of reality. Reality is one; it does not admit multiplicity or division. Reality is as the sun, which shines forth from different dawning points; it is as the light, which has illumined many lanterns.

Therefore, if the religions investigate reality and seek the essential truth of their own foundations, they will agree and no difference will be found. But inasmuch as religions are submerged in dogmatic imitations, forsaking the original foundations, and as imitations differ widely, therefore, the religions are divergent and antagonistic. These imitations may be likened to clouds which obscure the sunrise; but reality is the sun. If the clouds disperse, the Sun of Reality shines upon all, and no difference of vision will exist. The religions will then agree, for fundamentally they are the same. The subject is one, but predicates are many.

The divine religions are like the progression of the seasons of the year. When the earth becomes dead and desolate and because of frost and cold no trace of vanished spring remains, the springtime dawns again and clothes everything with a new garment of life. The meadows become fresh and green, the trees are adorned with verdure and fruits appear upon them. Then the winter comes again, and all the traces of spring disappear. This is the continuous cycle of the seasons—spring, winter, then the return of spring. But though the calendar changes and the years move forward, each springtime that comes is the return of the springtime that has gone; this spring is the renewal of the former spring. Springtime is springtime, no matter when or how often it comes. The divine Prophets are as the coming of spring, each renewing and quickening the teachings of the Prophet Who came before Him. Just as all seasons of spring are essentially one as to newness of life, vernal showers and beauty, so the essence of the mission and accomplishment of all the Prophets is one and the same. Now the people of religion have lost sight of the essential reality of the spiritual springtime. They have held tenaciously to ancestral forms and imitations, and because of this there is variance, strife and altercation among them. Therefore, we must now abandon these imitations and seek the foundation of the divine teachings; and inasmuch as the foundation is one reality, the divergent religionists must agree in it so that love and unity will be established among all people and denominations.

At a time when the Orient was rent by religious dissension Bahá'u'lláh appeared. He founded teachings which became the means of uniting the various and divergent peoples. He promulgated principles which removed the cause of their dissension, until today in Persia those who had been constantly at war are united. Christians, Muslims, Zoroastrians, Jews—people of every belief and denomination who have followed the teachings of Bahá'u'lláh—have attained complete fellowship and spiritual agreement. Former differences and dissensions have passed away entirely. Some of the principles of Bahá'u'lláh's teaching are as follows:

First, that the oneness of humanity shall be recognized and established. All men are the servants of God. He has created all; He is the Provider and Preserver; He is loving to all. Inasmuch as He is just and kind, why should we be unjust toward each other? As God has quickened us with life, why should we be the cause of death? As He has comforted us, why should we be the cause of anxiety and suffering? Can humanity conceive a plan and policy better and superior to that of God? It is certain that no matter how capable man may be in origination of plan and organization of purpose, his efforts will be inadequate when compared with the divine plan and purpose; for the policy of God is perfect. Therefore, we must follow the will and plan of God. As He is kind to all, we must be likewise; and it is certain that this will be most acceptable to God.

Second, that truth or reality must be investigated; for reality is one, and by investigating it all will find love and unity. Those who are ignorant must be educated, the ailing must be healed, the undeveloped must be brought to maturity. Shall we reject or oppose the ignorant, sick or immature because of their incapacity? Is it not better to be kind and gentle and to provide the means of remedy? Therefore, under no circumstances whatsoever should we assume any attitude except that of gentleness and humility.

Third, that religion is in harmony with science. The fundamental principles of the Prophets are scientific, but the forms and imitations which have appeared are opposed to science. If religion does not agree with science, it is superstition and ignorance; for God has endowed man with reason in order that he may perceive reality. The foundations of religion are reasonable. God has created us with intelligence to perceive them. If they are opposed to science and reason, how could they be believed and followed?

Fourth, that religion must be conducive to love and unity among mankind; for if it be the cause of enmity and strife, the absence of religion is preferable. When Moses appeared, the tribes of Israel were in a state of disunion as captives of the Pharaohs. Moses gathered them together, and the divine law established fellowship among them. They became as one people, united, consolidated, after which they were rescued from bondage. They passed into the promised land, advanced in all degrees, developed sciences and arts, progressed in material affairs, increased in divine or spiritual civilization until their nation rose to its zenith in the sovereignty of Solomon. It is evident, therefore, that religion is the cause of unity, fellowship and progress among mankind. The function of a shepherd is to gather the sheep together and not to scatter them. Then Christ appeared. He united varying and divergent creeds and warring people of His time. He brought together Greeks and Romans, reconciled Egyptians and Assyrians, Chaldeans and Phoenicians. Christ established unity and agreement among people of these hostile and warring nations. Therefore, it is again evident that the purpose of religion is peace and concord. Likewise, Muḥammad appeared at a time when the peoples and tribes of Arabia were divergent and in a state of continual warfare. They killed each other, pillaged and took captive wives and children. Muḥammad united these fierce tribes, established a foundation of fellowship among them so that they gave up warring against each other absolutely and established communities. The result was that the Arabian tribes freed themselves from the Persian yoke and Roman control, established an independent sovereignty which rose to a high degree of civilization, advanced in sciences and arts, extended the Saracen dominion as far west as Spain and Andalusia and became famous throughout the world. Therefore, it is proved once more that the religion of God is intended to be the cause of advancement and solidarity and not of enmity and dissolution. If it becomes the cause of hatred and strife, its absence is preferable. Its purpose is unity, and its foundations are one.

When Bahá'u'lláh appeared in Persia, violent strife and hatred separated the peoples and tribes of that country. They would not come together for any purpose except war; they would not partake of the same food, or drink of the same water; association and intercourse were impossible. Bahá'u'lláh founded the oneness of humanity among these people and bound their hearts together with such ties of love that they were completely united. He reestablished the prophetic foundations, reformed and renewed the principles laid down by the Messengers of God who had preceded Him. And now it is hoped that through His life and teachings the East and West shall become so united that no trace of enmity, strife and discord shall remain.

24 May 1912

TALK AT FREE RELIGIOUS ASSOCIATION, OR UNITARIAN CONFERENCE

Boston, Massachusetts

From Stenographic Notes

Creation is the expression of motion. Motion is life. A moving object is a living object, whereas that which is motionless and inert is as dead. All created forms are progressive in their planes, or kingdoms of existence, under the stimulus of the power or spirit of life. The universal energy is dynamic. Nothing is stationary in the material world of outer phenomena or in the inner world of intellect and consciousness.

Religion is the outer expression of the divine reality. Therefore, it must be living, vitalized, moving and progressive. If it be without motion and nonprogressive, it is without the divine life; it is dead. The divine institutes are continuously active and evolutionary; therefore, the revelation of them must be progressive and continuous. All things are subject to reformation. This is a century of life and renewal. Sciences and arts, industry and invention have been reformed. Law and ethics have been reconstituted, reorganized. The world of thought has been regenerated. Sciences of former ages and philosophies of the past are useless today. Present exigencies demand new methods of solution; world problems are without precedent. Old ideas and modes of thought are fast becoming obsolete. Ancient laws and archaic ethical systems will not meet the requirements of modern conditions, for this is clearly the century of a new life, the century of the revelation of reality and, therefore, the greatest of all centuries. Consider how the scientific developments of fifty years have surpassed and eclipsed the knowledge and achievements of all the former ages combined. Would the announcements and theories of ancient astronomers explain our present knowledge of the suns and planetary systems? Would the mask of obscurity which beclouded medieval centuries meet the demand for clear-eyed vision and understanding which characterizes the world today? Will the despotism of former governments answer the call for freedom which has risen from the heart of humanity in this cycle of illumination? It is evident that no vital results are now forthcoming from the customs, institutions and standpoints of the past. In view of this, shall blind imitations of ancestral forms and theological interpretations continue to guide and control the religious life and spiritual development of humanity today? Shall man, gifted with the power of reason, unthinkingly follow and adhere to dogma, creeds and hereditary beliefs which will not bear the analysis of reason in this century of effulgent reality? Unquestionably this will not satisfy men of science, for when they find premise or conclusion contrary to present standards of proof and without real foundation, they reject that which has been formerly accepted as standard and correct and move forward from new foundations.

The divine Prophets have revealed and founded religion. They have laid down certain laws and heavenly principles for the guidance of mankind. They have taught and promulgated the knowledge of God, established praiseworthy ethical ideals and inculcated the highest standards of virtues in the human world. Gradually these heavenly teachings and foundations of reality have been beclouded by human interpretations and dogmatic imitations of ancestral beliefs. The essential realities, which the Prophets labored so hard to establish in human hearts and minds while undergoing ordeals and suffering tortures of persecution, have now well nigh vanished. Some of these heavenly Messengers have been killed, some imprisoned, all of Them despised and rejected while proclaiming the reality of Divinity. Soon after Their departure from this world, the essential truth of Their teachings was lost sight of and dogmatic imitations adhered to.

Inasmuch as human interpretations and blind imitations differ widely, religious strife and disagreement have arisen among mankind, the light of true religion has been extinguished and the unity of the world of humanity destroyed. The Prophets of God voiced the spirit of unity and agreement. They have been the Founders of divine reality. Therefore, if the nations of the world forsake imitations and investigate the reality underlying the revealed Word of God, they will agree and become reconciled. For reality is one and not multiple.

The nations and religions are steeped in blind and bigoted imitations. A man is a Jew because his father was a Jew. The Muslim follows implicitly the footsteps of his ancestors in belief and observance. The Buddhist is true to his heredity as a Buddhist. That is to say, they profess religious belief blindly and without investigation, making unity and agreement impossible. It is evident, therefore, that this condition will not be remedied without a reformation in the world of religion. In other words, the fundamental reality of the divine religions must be renewed, reformed, revoiced to mankind.

From the seed of reality religion has grown into a tree which has put forth leaves and branches, blossoms and fruit. After a time this tree has fallen into a condition of decay. The leaves and blossoms have withered and perished; the tree has become stricken and fruitless. It is not reasonable that man should hold to the old tree, claiming that its life forces are undiminished, its fruit unequaled, its existence eternal. The seed of reality must be sown again in human hearts in order that a new tree may grow therefrom and new divine fruits refresh the world. By this means the nations and peoples now divergent in religion will be brought into unity, imitations will be forsaken, and a universal brotherhood in reality itself will be established. Warfare and strife will cease among mankind; all will be reconciled as servants of God. For all are sheltered beneath the tree of His providence and mercy. God is kind to all; He is the giver of bounty to all alike, even as Jesus Christ has declared that God "sendeth rain on the just and on the unjust"—that is to say, the mercy of God is universal. All humanity is under the protection of His love and favor, and unto all He has pointed the way of guidance and progress. Progress is of two kinds: material and spiritual. The former is attained through observation of the surrounding existence and constitutes the foundation of civilization. Spiritual progress is through the breaths of the Holy Spirit and is the awakening of the conscious soul of man to perceive the reality of Divinity. Material progress ensures the happiness of the human world. Spiritual progress ensures the happiness and eternal continuance of the soul. The Prophets of God have founded the laws of divine civilization. They have been the root and fundamental source of all knowledge. They have established the principles of human brotherhood, of fraternity, which is of various kinds—such as the fraternity of family, of race, of nation and of ethical motives. These forms of fraternity, these bonds of brotherhood, are merely temporal and transient in association. They do not ensure harmony and are usually productive of disagreement. They do not prevent warfare and strife; on the contrary, they are selfish, restricted and fruitful causes of enmity and hatred among mankind. The spiritual brotherhood which is enkindled and established through the breaths of the Holy Spirit unites nations and removes the cause of warfare and strife. It transforms mankind into one great family and establishes the foundations of the oneness of humanity. It promulgates the spirit of international agreement and ensures universal peace. Therefore, we must investigate the foundation of this heavenly fraternity. We must forsake all imitations and promote the reality of the divine teachings. In accordance with these principles and actions and by the assistance of the Holy Spirit, both material and spiritual happiness shall become realized. Until all nations and peoples become united by the bonds of the Holy Spirit in this real fraternity, until national and international prejudices are effaced in the reality of this spiritual brotherhood, true progress, prosperity and lasting happiness will not be attained by man. This is the century of new and universal nationhood. Sciences have advanced; industries have progressed; politics have been reformed; liberty has been proclaimed; justice is awakening. This is the century of motion, divine stimulus and accomplishment, the century of human solidarity and altruistic service, the century of universal peace and the reality of the divine Kingdom.

28 MAY 1912

TALK AT RECEPTION AT METROPOLITAN TEMPLE

SEVENTH AVENUE AND FOURTEENTH STREET,
NEW YORK

Notes by Esther Foster

The Fatherhood of God, His loving-kindness and beneficence are apparent to all. In His mercy He provides fully and amply for His creatures, and if any soul sins, He does not suspend His bounty. All created things are visible manifestations of His Fatherhood, mercy and heavenly bestowals. Human brotherhood is, likewise, as clear and evident as the sun, for all are servants of one God, belong to one humankind, inhabit the same globe, are sheltered beneath the overshadowing dome of heaven and submerged in the sea of divine mercy. Human brotherhood and dependence exist because mutual helpfulness and cooperation are the two necessary principles underlying human welfare. This is the physical relationship of mankind. There is another brotherhood—the spiritual—which is higher, holier and superior to all others. It is heavenly; it emanates from the breaths of the Holy Spirit and the effulgence of merciful attributes; it is founded upon spiritual susceptibilities. This brotherhood is established by the Manifestations of the Holy One.

The divine Manifestations since the day of Adam have striven to unite humanity so that all may be accounted as one soul. The function and purpose of a shepherd is to gather and not disperse his flock. The Prophets of God have been divine Shepherds of humanity. They have established a bond of love and unity among mankind, made scattered peoples one nation and wandering tribes a mighty kingdom. They have laid the foundation of the oneness of God and summoned all to universal peace. All these holy, divine Manifestations are one. They have served one God, promulgated the same truth, founded the same institutions and reflected the same light. Their appearances have been successive and correlated; each One has announced and extolled the One Who was to follow, and all laid the foundation of reality. They summoned and invited the people to love and made the human world a mirror of the Word of God. Therefore, the divine religions They established have one foundation; Their teachings, proofs and evidences are one; in name and form They differ, but in reality They agree and are the same. These holy Manifestations have been as the coming of springtime in the world. Although the springtime of this year is designated by another name according to the changing calendar, yet as regards its life and quickening it is the same as the springtime of last year. For each spring is the time of a new creation, the effects, bestowals, perfections and life-giving forces of which are the same as those of the former vernal seasons, although the names are many and various. This is 1912, last year was 1911 and so on, but in fundamental reality no difference is apparent. The sun is one, but the dawning points of the sun are numerous and changing. The ocean is one body of water, but different parts of it have particular designations—Atlantic,

Pacific, Mediterranean, Antarctic, etc. If we consider the names, there is differentiation; but the water, the ocean itself, is one reality.

Likewise, the divine religions of the holy Manifestations of God are in reality one, though in name and nomenclature they differ. Man must be a lover of the light, no matter from what dayspring it may appear. He must be a lover of the rose, no matter in what soil it may be growing. He must be a seeker of the truth, no matter from what source it come. Attachment to the lantern is not loving the light. Attachment to the earth is not befitting, but enjoyment of the rose which develops from the soil is worthy. Devotion to the tree is profitless, but partaking of the fruit is beneficial. Luscious fruits, no matter upon what tree they grow or where they may be found, must be enjoyed. The word of truth, no matter which tongue utters it, must be sanctioned. Absolute verities, no matter in what book they be recorded, must be accepted. If we harbor prejudice, it will be the cause of deprivation and ignorance. The strife between religions, nations and races arises from misunderstanding. If we investigate the religions to discover the principles underlying their foundations, we will find they agree; for the fundamental reality of them is one and not multiple. By this means the religionists of the world will reach their point of unity and reconciliation. They will ascertain the truth that the purpose of religion is the acquisition of praiseworthy virtues, the betterment of morals, the spiritual development of mankind, the real life and divine bestowals. All the Prophets have been the promoters of these principles; none of Them has been the promoter of corruption, vice or evil. They have summoned mankind to all good. They have united people in the love of God, invited them to the religions of the unity of mankind and exhorted them to amity and agreement. For example, we mention Abraham and Moses. By this mention we do not mean the limitation implied in the mere names but intend the virtues which these names embody. When we say Abraham, we mean thereby a manifestation of divine guidance, a center of human virtues, a source of heavenly bestowals to mankind, a dawning point of divine inspiration and perfections. These perfections and graces are not limited to names and boundaries. When we find these virtues, qualities and attributes in any personality, we recognize the same reality shining from within and bow in acknowledgment of the Abrahamic perfections. Similarly, we acknowledge and adore the beauty of Moses. Some souls were lovers of the name Abraham, loving the lantern instead of the light, and when they saw this same light shining from another lantern, they were so attached to the former lantern that they did not recognize its later appearance and illumination. Therefore, those who were attached and held tenaciously to the name Abraham were deprived when the Abrahamic virtues reappeared in Moses. Similarly, the Jews were believers in Moses, awaiting the coming of the Messiah. The virtues and perfections of Moses became apparent in Jesus Christ most effulgently, but the Jews held to the name Moses, not adoring the virtues and perfections manifest in Him. Had they been adoring these virtues and seeking these perfections, they would assuredly have believed in Jesus Christ when the same virtues and perfections shone in Him. If we are lovers of the light, we adore it in whatever lamp it may become manifest, but if we love the lamp itself and the light is transferred to another lamp, we will neither accept nor sanction it. Therefore, we must follow and adore the virtues revealed in the Messengers of God—whether in Abraham, Moses, Jesus or other Prophets—but we must not adhere to and adore the lamp. We must recognize the sun, no matter from what dawning point it may shine forth, be it Mosaic, Abrahamic or any personal point of orientation whatever, for we are lovers of sunlight and not of orientation. We are lovers of illumination and not of lamps and candles. We are seekers for water, no matter from what rock it may gush forth. We are in need of fruit in whatsoever orchard it may be ripened. We long for rain; it matters not which cloud pours it down. We must not be fettered. If we renounce these fetters, we shall agree, for all are seekers of reality. The counterfeit or imitation of true religion has adulterated human belief, and the foundations have been lost sight of. The variance of these imitations has produced enmity and strife, war and bloodshed. Now the glorious and brilliant twentieth century has dawned, and the divine bounty is radiating universally. The Sun of Truth is shining forth in intense enkindlement. This is, verily, the century when these imitations must be forsaken, superstitions abandoned and God alone worshiped. We must look at the reality of the Prophets and Their teachings in order that we may agree.

Praise be to God! The springtime of God is at hand. This century is, verily, the spring season. The world of mind and kingdom of soul have become fresh and verdant by its bestowals. It has resuscitated the whole realm of existence. On one hand, the lights of reality are shining; on the other, the clouds of divine mercy are pouring down the fullness of heavenly bounty. Wonderful material progress is evident, and great spiritual discoveries are being made. Truly, this can be called the miracle of centuries, for it is replete with manifestations of the miraculous. The time has come when all mankind shall be united, when all races shall be loyal to one fatherland, all religions become one religion, and racial and religious bias pass away. It is a day in which the oneness of humankind shall uplift its standard and international peace, like the true morning, flood the world with its light. Therefore, we offer supplications to God, asking Him to dispel these gloomy clouds and uproot these imitations in order that the East and West may become radiant with love and unity, that the nations of the world shall embrace each other and the ideal spiritual brotherhood illumine the world like the glorious sun of the high heavens. This is our hope, our wish and desire. We pray that through the bounty and grace of God we may attain thereto. I am very happy to be present at this meeting which has innate radiance, intelligence, perception and longing to investigate reality. Such meetings are the glory of the world of mankind. I ask the blessing of God in your behalf.

2 JUNE 1912

TALK AT CHURCH OF THE ASCENSION

FIFTH AVENUE AND TENTH STREET,
NEW YORK

Notes by Esther Foster

In the terminology of the Holy Books the church has been called the house of the covenant for the reason that the church is a place where people of different thoughts and divergent tendencies—where all races and nations—may come together in a covenant of permanent fellowship. In the temple of the Lord, in the house of God, man must be submissive to God. He must enter into a covenant with his Lord in order that he shall obey the divine commands and become unified with his fellowman. He must not consider divergence of races nor difference of nationalities; he must not view variation in denomination and creed, nor should he take into account the differing degrees of thoughts; nay, rather, he should look upon all as mankind and realize that all must become united and agreed. He must recognize all as one family, one race, one native land; he must see all as the servants of one God, dwelling beneath the shelter of His mercy. The purport of this is that the church is a collective center. Temples are symbols of the reality and divinity of God—the collective center of mankind. Consider how within a temple every race and people is seen and represented—all in the presence of the Lord, covenanting together in a covenant of love and fellowship, all offering the same melody, prayer and supplication to God. Therefore, it is evident that the church is a collective center for mankind. For this reason there have been churches and temples in all the divine religions; but the real Collective Centers are the Manifestations of God, of Whom the church or temple is a symbol and expression. That is to say, the Manifestation of God is the real divine temple and Collective Center of which the outer church is but a symbol.

Recall the statement of Jesus Christ in the Gospel. Addressing Peter, He said, "Thou art Peter, and upon this rock I will build my church." It is evident, therefore, that the church of God is the law of God and that the actual edifice is but one symbol thereof. For the law of God is a collective center which unites various peoples, native lands, tongues and opinions. All find shelter in its protection and become attracted by it. For example, Moses and the Mosaic law were the unifying center for the scattered sheep of Israel. He united these wandering flocks, brought them under control of divine law, educated and unified them, caused them to agree and uplifted them to a superlative degree of development. At a time when they were debased, they became glorified; ignorant, they were made knowing; in the bonds of captivity, they were given freedom; in short, they were unified. Day by day they advanced until they attained the highest degree of progress witnessed in that age. We prove, therefore, that the Manifestation of God and the law of God accomplish unity.

It is self-evident that humanity is at variance. Human tastes differ; thoughts, native lands, races and tongues are many. The need of a collective center by which these differences may be counterbalanced and the people of the world be unified is obvious. Consider how nothing but a spiritual power can bring about this unification, for material conditions and mental aspects are so widely different that agreement and unity are not possible through outer means. It is possible, however, for all to become unified through one spirit, just as all may receive light from one sun. Therefore, assisted by the collective and divine center which is the law of God and the reality of His Manifestation, we can overcome these conditions until they pass away entirely and the races advance.

Consider the time of Christ. Peoples, races and governments were many; religions, sects and denominations were various; but when Christ appeared, the Messianic reality proved to be the collective center which unified them beneath the same tabernacle of agreement. Reflect upon this. Could Jesus Christ have united these divergent factors or brought about such results through political power? Was this unity and agreement possible through material forces? It is evident that it was not; nay, rather, these various peoples were brought together through a divine power, through the breaths of the Holy Spirit. They were blended and quickened by the infusion of a new life. The spirituality of Christ overcame their difficulties so that their disagreements passed away completely. In this way these divergent peoples were unified and became welded in a bond of love which alone can unite hearts. Therefore, it is shown that the di-

vine Manifestations, the holy Mouthpieces of God,
are the Collective Centers of God. These heavenly
Messengers are the real Shepherds of humanity, for
whenever They appear in the world They unite the
scattered sheep. The Collective Center has always appeared in the Orient. Abraham, Moses, Jesus Christ,
Muḥammad were Collective Centers of Their day
and time, and all arose in the East. Today Bahá'u'lláh
is the Collective Center of unity for all mankind, and
the splendor of His light has likewise dawned from
the East. He founded the oneness of humanity in Persia. He established harmony and agreement among
the various peoples of religious beliefs, denominations, sects and cults by freeing them from the fetters of past imitations and superstitions, leading them
to the very foundation of the divine religions. From
this foundation shines forth the radiance of spirituality, which is unity, the love of God, the knowledge
of God, praiseworthy morals and the virtues of the
human world. Bahá'u'lláh renewed these principles,
just as the coming of spring refreshes the earth and
confers new life upon all phenomenal beings. For the
freshness of the former springtimes had waned, the
vivification had ceased, the life-giving breezes were no
longer wafting their fragrances, winter and the season
of darkness had come. Bahá'u'lláh came to renew the
life of the world with this new and divine springtime,
which has pitched its tent in the countries of the Orient in the utmost power and glory. It has refreshed
the world of the Orient, and there is no doubt that
if the world of the Occident should abandon dog-

mas of the past, turn away from empty imitations and superstitions, investigate the reality of the divine religions, holding fast to the example of Jesus Christ, acting in accordance with the teachings of God and becoming unified with the Orient, an eternal happiness and felicity would be attained.

In the western world material civilization has attained the highest point of development, but divine civilization was founded in the land of the East. The East must acquire material civilization from the West, and the West must receive spiritual civilization from the East. This will establish a mutual bond. When these two come together, the world of humanity will present a glorious aspect, and extraordinary progress will be achieved. This is clear and evident; no proof is needed. The degree of material civilization in the Occident cannot be denied; nor can anyone fail to confirm the spiritual civilization of the Orient, for all the divine foundations of human uplift have appeared in the East. This, likewise, is clear and evident. Therefore, you must assist the East in order that it may attain material progress. The East must, likewise, promulgate the principles of spiritual civilization in the western world. By this commingling and union the human race will attain the highest degree of prosperity and development. Material civilization alone is not sufficient and will not prove productive. The physical happiness of material conditions was allotted to the animal. Consider how the animal has attained the fullest degree of physical felicity. A bird perches upon the loftiest branch and builds there its nest with consummate beauty and skill. All the grains and seeds of the meadows are its wealth and food; all the fresh water of mountain springs and rivers of the plain are for its enjoyment. Truly, this is the acme of material happiness, to which even a human creature cannot attain. This is the honor of the animal kingdom. But the honor of the human kingdom is the attainment of spiritual happiness in the human world, the acquisition of the knowledge and love of God. The honor allotted to man is the acquisition of the supreme virtues of the human world. This is his real happiness and felicity. But if material happiness and spiritual felicity be conjoined, it will be "delight upon delight," as the Arabs say. We pray that God will unite the East and the West in order that these two civilizations may be exchanged and mutually enjoyed. I am sure it will come to pass, for this is the radiant century. This is an age for the outpouring of divine mercy upon the exigency of this new century—the unity of the East and the West. It will surely be accomplished.

9 June 1912

———————————

TALK AT UNITARIAN CHURCH

———————————

Fifteenth Street and Girard Avenue,
Philadelphia, Pennsylvania

Notes by Edna McKinney

I have come from distant countries of the Orient where the lights of heaven have ever shone forth, from regions where the Manifestations of God have appeared and the radiance and power of God have been revealed to mankind. The purpose and intention of my visit is that, perchance, a bond of unity and agreement may be established between the East and West, that divine love may encompass all nations, divine radiance enlighten both continents and the bounties of the Holy Spirit revivify the body of the world. Therefore, I supplicate the threshold of God that the Orient and Occident may become as one, that the various peoples and religions be unified and souls be blended as the waves of one sea. May they become as trees, flowers and roses which adorn and beautify the same garden.

The realm of Divinity is an indivisible oneness, wholly sanctified above human comprehension; for intellectual knowledge of creation is finite, whereas comprehension of Divinity is infinite. How can the finite comprehend the infinite? We are utter poverty, whereas the reality of Divinity is absolute wealth. How can utter poverty understand absolute wealth? We are utter weakness, whereas the reality of Divinity is absolute power. Utter weakness can never attain nor apprehend absolute power. The phenomenal beings, which are captives of limitations, are ever subject to transformation and change in condition. How can such phenomenal beings ever grasp the heavenly, eternal, unchanging reality? Assuredly this is an absolute impossibility, for when we study the creational world, we see that the difference of degree is a barrier to such knowing. An inferior degree can never comprehend a higher degree or kingdom. The mineral, no matter how far it may advance, can never attain knowledge of the vegetable. No matter how the plant or vegetable may progress, it cannot perceive the reality of the animal kingdom—in other words, it cannot grasp a world of life that is endowed with the power of the senses. The animal may develop a wonderful degree of intelligence, but it can never attain the powers of ideation and conscious reflection which belong to man. It is evident, therefore, that difference in degree is ever an obstacle to comprehension of the higher by the lower, the superior by the inferior. This flower, so beautiful, fresh, fragrant and delicately scented, although it may have attained perfection in its own kingdom, nevertheless cannot comprehend the human reality, cannot possess sight and hearing; therefore, it exists unaware of the world of man, although man and itself are both accidental or conditional beings. The difference is difference of degree. The limitation of an inferior degree is the barrier to comprehension.

This being so, how can the human reality, which is limited, comprehend the eternal, unmanifest Creator? How can man comprehend the omniscient, omnipresent Lord? Undoubtedly, he cannot, for whatever comes within the grasp of human mind is man's limited conception, whereas the divine Kingdom is unlimited, infinite. But although the reality of Divinity is sanctified beyond the comprehension of its creatures, it has bestowed its bounties upon all kingdoms of the phenomenal world, and evidences of spiritual manifestation are witnessed throughout the realms of contingent existence. The lights of God illumine the world of man, even as the effulgences of the sun shine gloriously upon the material creation. The Sun of Reality is one; its bestowal is one; its heat is one; its rays are one; it shines upon all the phenomenal world, but the capacity for comprehending it differs according to the kingdoms, each kingdom receiving the light and bounty of the eternal Sun according to its capacity. The black stone receives the light of the material sun; the trees and animals likewise are recipients of it. All exist and are developed by that one bounty. The perfect soul of man—that is to say, the perfect individual—is like a mirror wherein the Sun of Reality is reflected. The perfections, the image and light of that Sun have been revealed in the mirror; its heat and illumination are manifest therein, for that pure soul is a perfect expression of the Sun.

These mirrors are the Messengers of God Who tell the story of Divinity, just as the material mirror reflects the light and disc of the outer sun in the skies. In this way the image and effulgence of the Sun of Reality appear in the mirrors of the Manifestations of God. This is what Jesus Christ meant when He declared, "the father is in the son," the purpose being that the reality of that eternal Sun had become reflected in its glory in Christ Himself. It does not signify that the Sun of Reality had descended from its place in heaven or that its essential being had effected an entrance into the mirror, for there is neither entrance nor exit for the reality of Divinity; there is no ingress or egress; it is sanctified above all things and ever occupies its own holy station. Changes and transformations are not applicable to that eternal reality. Transformation from condition to condition is the attribute of contingent realities.

At a time when warfare and strife prevailed among nations, when enmity and hatred separated sects and denominations and human differences were very great, Bahá'u'lláh appeared upon the horizon of the East, proclaiming the oneness of God and the unity of the world of humanity. He promulgated the teaching that all mankind are the servants of one God; that all have come into being through the bestowal of the one Creator; that God is kind to all, nurtures, rears and protects all, provides for all and extends His love and mercy to all races and people. Inasmuch as God is loving, why should we be unjust and unkind? As God manifests loyalty and mercy, why should we show forth enmity and hatred? Surely the divine policy is more perfect than human plan and theory; for no matter how wise and sagacious man may become, he can never attain a policy that is superior to the policy of God. Therefore, we must emulate the attitude of God, love all people, be just and kind to every human creature. We must consider all as the leaves, branches and fruit of one tree, children of one household; for all are the progeny of Adam. We are waves of one sea, grass of the same meadow, stars in the same heaven; and we find shelter in the universal divine Protector. If one be sick, he must be treated; the ignorant must be educated; the sleeping must be awakened; the dead must be quickened with life. These were principles of the teachings of Bahá'u'lláh.

In proclaiming the oneness of mankind He taught that men and women are equal in the sight of God and that there is no distinction to be made between them. The only difference between them now is due to lack of education and training. If woman is given equal opportunity of education, distinction and estimate of inferiority will disappear. The world of humanity has two wings, as it were: One is the female; the other is the male. If one wing be defective, the strong perfect wing will not be capable of flight. The world of humanity has two hands. If one be imperfect, the capable hand is restricted and unable to perform its duties. God is the Creator of mankind. He has endowed both sexes with perfections and intelligence, given them physical members and organs of sense, without differentiation or distinction as to superiority; therefore, why should woman be considered inferior? This is not according to the plan and justice of God. He has created them equal; in His estimate there is no question of sex. The one whose heart is purest, whose deeds are most perfect, is acceptable to God, male or female. Often in history women have been the pride of humanity—for example, Mary, the mother of Jesus. She was the glory of mankind. Mary Magdalene, Ásíyih, daughter of Pharaoh, Sarah, wife of Abraham, and innumerable others have glorified the human race by their excellences. In this day there are women among the Bahá'ís who far outshine men. They are wise, talented, well-informed, progressive, most intelligent and the light of men. They surpass men in courage. When they speak in meetings, the men listen with great respect. Furthermore, the education of women is of greater importance than the education of men, for they are the mothers of the race, and mothers rear the children. The first teachers of children are the mothers. Therefore, they must be capably trained in order to educate both sons and daughters. There are many provisions in the words of Bahá'u'lláh in regard to this.

He promulgated the adoption of the same course of education for man and woman. Daughters and sons must follow the same curriculum of study, thereby promoting unity of the sexes. When all mankind shall receive the same opportunity of education and the equality of men and women be realized, the foundations of war will be utterly destroyed. Without equality this will be impossible because all differences and distinction are conducive to discord and strife. Equality between men and women is conducive to the abolition of warfare for the reason that women will never be willing to sanction it. Mothers will not give their sons as sacrifices upon the battlefield after twenty years of anxiety and loving devotion in rear-ing them from infancy, no matter what cause they are called upon to defend. There is no doubt that when women obtain equality of rights, war will entirely cease among mankind.

Bahá'u'lláh promulgated the fundamental oneness of religion. He taught that reality is one and not multiple, that it underlies all divine precepts and that the foundations of the religions are, therefore, the same. Certain forms and imitations have gradually arisen. As these vary, they cause differences among religionists. If we set aside these imitations and seek the fundamental reality underlying our beliefs, we reach a basis of agreement because it is one and not multiple.

Among other principles of Bahá'u'lláh's teachings was the harmony of science and religion. Religion must stand the analysis of reason. It must agree with scientific fact and proof so that science will sanction religion and religion fortify science. Both are indissolubly welded and joined in reality. If statements and teachings of religion are found to be unreasonable and contrary to science, they are outcomes of superstition and imagination. Innumerable doctrines and beliefs of this character have arisen in the past ages. Consider the superstitions and mythology of the Romans, Greeks and Egyptians; all were contrary to religion and science. It is now evident that the beliefs of these nations were superstitions, but in those times they held to them most tenaciously. For example, one of the many Egyptian idols was to those people an authenticated miracle, whereas in reality it was a piece of stone. As science could not sanction the miraculous origin and nature of a piece of rock, the belief in it must have been superstition. It is now evident that it was superstition. Therefore, we must cast aside such beliefs and investigate reality. That which is found to be real and conformable to reason must be accepted, and whatever science and reason cannot support must be rejected as imitation and not reality. Then differences of belief will disappear. All will become as one family, one people, and the same susceptibility to the divine bounty and education will be witnessed among mankind.

O Thou forgiving Lord! Thou art the shelter of all these Thy servants. Thou knowest the secrets and art aware of all things. We are all helpless, and Thou art the Mighty, the Omnipotent. We are all sinners, and Thou art the Forgiver of sins, the Merciful, the Compassionate. O Lord! Look not at our shortcomings. Deal with us according to Thy grace and bounty. Our shortcomings are many, but the ocean of Thy forgiveness is boundless. Our weakness is grievous, but the evidences of Thine aid and assistance are clear. Therefore, confirm and strengthen us. Enable us to do that which is worthy of Thy holy Threshold. Illumine our hearts, grant us discerning eyes and attentive ears. Resuscitate the dead and heal the sick. Bestow wealth upon the poor and give peace and security to the fearful. Accept us in Thy kingdom and illumine us with the light of guidance. Thou art the Powerful and the Omnipotent. Thou art the Generous. Thou art the Clement. Thou art the Kind.

25 September 1912

———————————

TALK AT SECOND DIVINE SCIENCE CHURCH

———————————

3929 West Thirty-eighth Avenue,
Denver, Colorado

From Stenographic Notes

In the Orient I was informed of the lofty purposes and wonderful attainments of the American people. When I arrived in this country, I realized that American ideals are indeed most praiseworthy and that the people here are lovers of truth. They investigate reality, and there is no trace of fanaticism among them. Today the nations of the world are on the verge of war, influenced and impelled by prejudices of ignorance and racial fanaticism. Praise be to God! You are free from such prejudice, for you believe in the oneness and solidarity of the world of humanity. There is no doubt that the divine confirmations will uphold you.

One of the forms of prejudice which afflict the world of mankind is religious bigotry and fanaticism. When this hatred burns in human hearts, it becomes the cause of revolution, destruction, abasement of humankind and deprivation of the mercy of God. For the holy Manifestations and divine Founders of religion Themselves were completely unified in love and agreement, whereas Their followers are characterized by bitter antagonism and attitudes of hostility toward each other. God has desired for mankind the effulgence of love, but through blindness and misapprehension man has enveloped himself in veils of discord, strife and hatred. The supreme need of humanity is cooperation and reciprocity. The stronger the ties of fellowship and solidarity amongst men, the greater will be the power of constructiveness and accomplishment in all the planes of human activity. Without cooperation and reciprocal attitude the individual member of human society remains self-centered, uninspired by altruistic purposes, limited and solitary in development like the animal and plant organisms of the lower kingdoms. The lower creatures are not in need of cooperation and reciprocity. A tree can live solitary and alone, but this is impossible for man without retrogression. Therefore, every cooperative attitude and activity of human life is praiseworthy and forelintended by the will of God. The first expression of cooperation is family relationship, which is unreliable and uncertain in its potency, for it is subject to separation and does not permanently cement together the individual members of humanity. There is also a cooperation and oneness in nativity or race which is likewise not efficient, for although its members may agree in general, they differ radically in personal and particular points of view. Racial association, therefore, will not ensure the requirements of divine relationship. There are other means in the human world by which physical association is established, but these fail to weld together the hearts and spirits of men and are correspondingly inefficient. Therefore, it is evident that God has destined and intended religion to be the cause and means of cooperative effort and accomplishment among mankind. To this end He has sent the Prophets of God, the holy Manifestations of the Word, in order that the fundamental reality and religion of God may prove to be the bond of human unity, for the divine religions revealed by these holy Messengers have one and the same foundation. All will admit, therefore, that the divine religions are intended to be the means of true human cooperation, that they are united in the purpose of making humanity one family, for they rest upon the universal foundation of love, and love is the first effulgence of Divinity.

Each one of the divine religions has established two kinds of ordinances: the essential and the accidental. The essential ordinances rest upon the firm, unchanging, eternal foundations of the Word itself. They concern spiritualities, seek to stabilize morals, awaken intuitive susceptibilities, reveal the knowledge of God and inculcate the love of all mankind. The accidental laws concern the administration of outer human actions and relations, establishing rules and regulations requisite for the world of bodies and their control. These are ever subject to change and supersedure according to exigencies of time, place and condition. For example, during the time of Moses, ten commandments concerning the punishment of murder were revealed in His Book. Divorce was sanctioned and polygamy allowable to a certain extent. If a man committed theft, his hand was cut off. This was drastic law and severe punishment applicable to the time of Moses. But when the time of Christ came, minds had developed, realizations were keener and spiritual perceptions had advanced so that certain laws concerning murder, plurality of wives and di-

vorce were abrogated. But the essential ordinances of
the Mosaic dispensation remained unchanged. These
were the fundamental realities of the knowledge of
God and the holy Manifestations, the purification
of morals, the awakening of spiritual susceptibilities—eternal principles in which there is no change
or transformation. Briefly, the foundation of the divine religions is one eternal foundation, but the laws
for temporary conditions and exigencies are subject to
change. Therefore, by adherence to these temporary
laws, blindly following and imitating ancestral forms,
difference and divergence have arisen among followers
of the various religions, resulting in disunion, strife
and hatred. Blind imitations and dogmatic observances are conducive to alienation and disagreement;
they lead to bloodshed and destruction of the foundations of humanity. Therefore, the religionists of the
world must lay aside these imitations and investigate
the essential foundation or reality itself, which is not
subject to change or transformation. This is the divine
means of agreement and unification.

The purpose of all the divine religions is the establishment of the bonds of love and fellowship among
men, and the heavenly phenomena of the revealed
Word of God are intended to be a source of knowledge and illumination to humanity. So long as man
persists in his adherence to ancestral forms and imitation of obsolete ceremonials, denying higher revelations of the divine light in the world, strife and
contention will destroy the purpose of religion and

make love and fellowship impossible. Each of the holy Manifestations announced the glad tidings of His successor, and each One confirmed the message of His predecessor. Therefore, inasmuch as They were agreed and united in purpose and teaching, it is incumbent upon Their followers to be likewise unified in love and spiritual fellowship. In no other way will discord and alienation disappear and the oneness of the world of humanity be established.

After we have proved the validity of the Manifestations of the Word of God by investigating the divine teachings, we must discover for a certainty whether They have been real Educators of mankind. Among the revelators of the law of God was Moses. When He appeared, all the contemporaneous nations rejected Him. Notwithstanding this, single and alone He promulgated the divine teachings and liberated a nation from the lowest condition of degradation and bondage. The people of Israel were ignorant, lowly, debased in morals—a race of slaves under burdensome oppression. Moses led them out of captivity and brought them to the Holy Land. He educated and disciplined them, established among them the foundations of material and divine civilization. Through the education of Moses these ignorant people attained an advanced degree of power and prestige, culminating in the glory of the reign of Solomon. From the abyss of bereavement and slavery they were uplifted to the highest plane of progress and civilized nationhood. It is evident, therefore, that Moses was an Educator and Teacher. The purpose and mission of the holy, divine Messengers is the training and advancement of humanity, the cultivation of divine fruits in the gardens of human hearts, the reflection of heavenly effulgence in the mirrors of human souls, the quickening of mental capacity and the increase of spiritual susceptibilities. When these results and outcomes are witnessed in mankind, the function and mission of the Manifestations are unmistakable. Christ, single and alone, without schooling or outward education and trained to labor in the shop of a carpenter, appeared in the world at the time when the Jewish nation was in the greatest abasement. This radiant Youth, without wealth, power of armies or prestige, rescued the Jews who believed on Him from tyranny and degradation and lifted them to the highest plane of development and glory. Peter, His disciple, was a fisherman. Through the power of Christ he shed light upon all the horizons of the world. Furthermore, various people of the Greek, Roman, Egyptian and Assyrian nations were brought together in unity and agreement; where warfare and bloodshed had existed, humility and love were manifest, and the foundations of divine religion were established, never to be destroyed. This proves that Christ was a heavenly Teacher and Educator of the world of humanity, for such evidences are historical and irrefutable, not based upon tradition and circumstantial report. The power of His Word in cementing these nations together is as clear and evident as the sun at midday. There is no need of further demonstration.

The proof of the validity of a Manifestation of God is the penetration and potency of His Word, the cultivation of heavenly attributes in the hearts and lives of His followers and the bestowal of divine education upon the world of humanity. This is absolute proof. The world is a school in which there must be Teachers of the Word of God. The evidence of the ability of these Teachers is efficient education of the graduating classes.

In the early part of the nineteenth century the horizon of Persia was shrouded in great darkness and ignorance. The people of that country were in a condition of barbarism. Hatred and bigotry prevailed among the various religions; bloodshed and hostility were frequent among sects and denominations of belief. There were no evidences of affiliation and unity; violent prejudice and antagonism ruled the hearts of men. At such a time as this Bahá'u'lláh proclaimed the first principle of His mission and teaching—the oneness of the world of humanity. His second announcement was the investigation of reality; the third was the oneness of the foundations of the divine religions. Through spiritual education He led the people out of darkness and ignorance into the clear light of truth, illuminated their hearts with the splendor of knowledge, laid a true and universal basis for religious teachings, cultivated the virtues of humanity, conferred spiritual susceptibilities, awakened inner perceptions and changed the dishonor of prejudiced souls to the highest degree of honor and capacity. Today in Persia and the Orient you will find the followers of Bahá'u'lláh united in the closest ties of fellowship and love. They have abandoned religious prejudices and have become as one family. When you enter their meetings, you will find Christians, Muslims, Buddhists, Zoroastrians, Jews and representatives of other beliefs present, all conjoined in a wonderful unity without a trace of bigotry or fanaticism, and the light of the oneness of the world of humanity reflected in their faces. Day by day they are advancing, manifesting greater and still greater love for each other. Their faith is fixed upon the unification of mankind, and their highest purpose is the oneness of religious belief. They proclaim to all humanity the sheltering mercy and infinite grace of God. They teach the reconciliation of religion with science and reason. They show forth in words and deeds the reality of love for all mankind as the servants of one God and the recipients of His universal bounty. These are their thoughts, their beliefs, their guiding principles, their religion. No trace of religious, racial, patriotic or political prejudice can be found among them, for they are real servants of God and obedient to His will and command.

My highest hope and desire is that the strongest and most indissoluble bond shall be established between the American nation and the people of the Orient. This is my prayer to God. May the day come when through divine and spiritual activity in the human world the religions shall be reconciled and all races of mankind come together in unity and love. Fifty years ago Bahá'u'lláh proclaimed the peace of the nations and oneness of the divine religions, addressing His words to all the kings and rulers of the world in specific Tablets. Therefore, my supreme desire is the unity of the East and West, universal peace and the oneness of the world of humanity.

7 OCTOBER 1912

———————————

TALK TO JAPANESE YOUNG MEN'S CHRISTIAN ASSOCIATION, JAPANESE INDEPENDENT CHURCH

———————————

OAKLAND, CALIFORNIA

Notes by Bijou Straun

It is a great happiness to be here this evening, especially for the reason that the members of this Association have come from the region of the Orient. For a long time I have entertained a desire to meet some of the Japanese friends. That nation has achieved extraordinary progress in a short space of time—a progress and development which have astonished the world. Inasmuch as they have advanced in material civilization, they must assuredly possess the capacity for spiritual development. For this reason, I have an excessive longing to meet them. Praise be to God! This pleasure is now afforded me, for here in this city I am face to face with a revered group of the Japanese. According to report the people of the Japanese nation are not prejudiced. They investigate reality. Wherever they find truth, they prove to be its lovers. They are not attached tenaciously to blind imitations of ancient beliefs and dogmas. Therefore, it is my great desire to discourse with them upon a subject in order that the unity and blending together of the nations of the East and the nations of the West may be furthered and accomplished. In this way religious, racial and political prejudice, partisan bias and sectarianism will be dispelled amongst men. Any kind of prejudice is destructive to the body politic.

When we review history from the beginning of human existence to the present age in which we live, it is evident all war and conflict, bloodshed and battle, every form of sedition has been due to some form of prejudice—whether religious, racial or national—to partisan bias and selfish prejudice of some sort. Even today we witness an upheaval in the Balkans, a war of religious prejudice. Some years ago when I was living in Rumelia, war broke out among the religious peoples. There was no attitude of justice or equity whatever amongst them. They pillaged the properties of each other, burning each others' homes and houses, slaughtering men, women and children, imagining that such warfare and bloodshed was the means of drawing near to God. This clearly proved that prejudice is a destroyer of the foundations of the world of humanity, whereas religion was meant to be the cause of fellowship and agreement.

Religion must be the cause of love. Religion must be the cause of justice, for the wisdom of the Manifestations of God is directed toward the establishing of the bond of a love which is indissoluble. The bonds which hold together the body politic are not sufficient. These bonds may be mentioned—for instance, the bond of patriotism. This is evidently not a sufficient bond, for how often it happens that people of the same nation wage civil war amongst themselves. The bond of fellowship may be racial, but history proves this is not sufficiently strong, for tremendous wars have broken out between peoples of the same racial lineage. Again, the bond holding men together may be political. How often it happens that the diplomacy of nations makes a treaty of peace one day and on the morrow a declaration of war! It is historically evident and manifest that these bonds are not self-sufficient.

The real bond of integrity is religious in character, for religion indicates the oneness of the world of humanity. Religion serves the world of morality. Religion purifies the hearts. Religion impels men to achieve praiseworthy deeds. Religion becomes the cause of love in human hearts, for religion is a divine foundation, the foundation ever conducive to life. The teachings of God are the source of illumination to the people of the world. Religion is ever constructive, not destructive.

The foundation of all the divine religions is one. All are based upon reality. Reality does not admit plurality, yet amongst mankind there have arisen differences concerning the Manifestations of God. Some have been Zoroastrians, some are Buddhists, some Jews, Christians, Muslims and so on. This has become a source of divergence, whereas the teachings of the holy Souls Who founded the divine religions are one in essence and reality. All these have served the world of humanity. All have summoned souls to peace and accord. All have proclaimed the virtues of humanity. All have guided souls to the attainment of perfections, but among the nations certain imitations of ancestral forms of worship have arisen. These imitations are not the foundation and essence of the divine religions. Inasmuch as they differ from the reality and the essential teachings of the Manifestations of

God, dissensions have arisen, and prejudice has developed. Religious prejudice thus becomes the cause of warfare and battle.

If we abandon these timeworn blind imitations and investigate reality, all of us will be unified. No discord will remain; antagonism will disappear. All will associate in fellowship. All will enjoy the cordial bonds of friendship. The world of creation will then attain composure. The dark and gloomy clouds of blind imitations and dogmatic variances will be scattered and dispelled; the Sun of Reality will shine most gloriously.

Verily, we should consider the divine Prophets as the intermediaries, but mankind has made use of Them as causes of dissension and pretexts for warfare and strife. In reality, They were the intermediaries of love and reconciliation. If They were not sources of love and fellowship amongst men, then undoubtedly They were not true, for the divine wisdom and purpose in sending the Prophets was the manifestation of love in human hearts. Therefore, we must investigate reality. First of all, let us determine whether these Prophets were valid or not by using rational proofs and shining arguments, not simply by quoting traditionary evidences, because traditions are divergent and the source of dissension.

Among the holy, divine Manifestations of God were Moses, Buddha, etc. The sending of Prophets has ever been for the training of humanity. They are the first Educators and Trainers. If Moses has developed the body politic, there is no doubt that He was a true Teacher and Educator. This will be proof and evidence that He was a Prophet. We shall consider how He was sent to the children of Israel when they were in the abyss of despair, in the lowest degree of ignorance and heedlessness, degraded and under conditions of bondage. Moses rescued these degraded people of Israel from that state of bondage. He raised them from that condition of ignorance, saved them from barbarism and led them into the Holy Land. He educated them, endowed them with sagacious instincts, made them worthy and honorable. He civilized them, raised them to a higher plane of existence until they were enabled to establish a national sovereignty, the great kingdom of Solomon. This proves that Moses was a Teacher and an Educator. He had neither army nor dominion; neither did He possess wealth. It was only through an idealistic power that He cemented them together, proving that He was a Prophet of God, an Educator and Trainer.

Likewise, must we set aside prejudice in considering other divine Educators by investigating reality. For instance, let us take Christ. He achieved results greater than Moses. He educated the body politic, trained mighty nations. There is no doubt whatever that such Souls were Prophets, for the mission of Prophethood is education, and these wondrous Souls trained and educated mankind.

Christ was a unique Personage, without helper or assistant. Single and solitary He arose to train great and mighty nations; the Romans, Greeks, Egyptians, Syrians, Chaldeans and Assyrians came under His influence. He was able to bind together many nations, melting them together, as it were, and pouring them into one mold, changing their enmity into love, war into peace. Under His influence satanic souls became veritable angels, tyrannical rulers became just, the human moral standard was raised. This proves that Christ was an Educator, a Teacher and Trainer of nations. If we deny this, it is nought but injustice.

Blessed souls—whether Moses, Jesus, Zoroaster, Krishna, Buddha, Confucius or Muḥammad—were the cause of the illumination of the world of humanity. How can we deny such irrefutable proof? How can we be blind to such light? How can we dispute the validity of Christ? This is injustice. This is a denial of reality. Man must be just. We must set aside bias and prejudice. We must abandon the imitations of ancestors and forefathers. We ourselves must investigate reality and be fair in judgment.

The old nation of Persia denied all these facts, harboring the utmost hatred and enmity toward other religious beliefs besides their own. We have investigated reality and found that these holy souls were all sent of God. All of them have sacrificed life, endured ordeals and tribulations in order that They might educate us. How can such love be forgotten? The light of Christ is evident. The candle of Buddha is shining. The star of Moses is sparkling. The flame ignited by Zoroaster is still burning. How can we deny Them? It is injustice. It is a denial of complete evidence. If we forsake imitations, all will become united, and no differences will remain to separate us.

We entertain no prejudice against Muḥammad.
Outwardly the Arabian nation was instrumental in
overthrowing the Pársí dominion, the sovereignty
of Persia. Therefore, the old Pársí nation manifested
the utmost contempt toward the Arabs. But we deal
justly and will never abandon the standard of fairness.
The Arabians were in the utmost state of degradation.
They were bloodthirsty and barbarous, so savage and
degraded that the Arabian father often buried his own
daughter alive. Consider: Could any barbarism be lower than this? The nation consisted of warring, hostile
tribal peoples inhabiting the vast Arabian peninsula,
and their business consisted in fighting and pillaging each other, making captive women and children,
killing each other. Muḥammad appeared among such
a people. He educated and unified these barbarous
tribes, put an end to their shedding of blood. Through
His education they reached such a degree of civilization that they subdued and governed continents and
nations. What a great civilization was established in
Spain by the Muslims! What a marvelous civilization
was founded in Morocco by the Moors! What a powerful caliphate or successorship was set up in Baghdád!
How much Islám served and furthered the cause of
science! Why then should we deny Muḥammad? If
we deny Him, we awaken enmity and hatred. By our
prejudice we become the cause of war and bloodshed,
for prejudice was the cause of the tremendous storm
which swept through human history for thirteen hundred years and still continues. Even now in the Balkans a commotion is apparent, reflecting it.

The Christian people number nearly three hundred millions and the Muslims about the same. It is no small task to do away with such numbers. And furthermore, why should they be obliterated? For these are all servants of the one God. Let us strive to establish peace between Christians and Muslims. Is it not better? What is the benefit of war? What is its fruitage? For thirteen hundred years there has been warfare and hostility. What good result has been forthcoming? Is it not folly? Is God pleased with it? Is Christ pleased? Is Muḥammad? It is evident that They are not. The Prophets have extolled each other to the utmost. Muḥammad declared Christ to be the Spirit of God. This is an explicit text of the Qur'án. He declared Christ to be the Word of God. He eulogized the disciples of Christ to the utmost. He bestowed upon Mary, the mother of Christ, the highest praise. Likewise, Christ extolled Moses. He spread broadcast the Old Testament, the Torah, and caused the name of Moses to reach unto the East and the West. The purpose is this: that the Prophets Themselves have manifested the utmost love toward each other, but the nations who believe and follow Them are hostile and antagonistic among themselves.

The world was in this condition of darkness when Bahá'u'lláh appeared upon the Persian horizon. He hoisted the banner of the oneness of the world of humanity. He proclaimed international peace. He admonished the Persian nation to investigate reality, announced that religion must be the cause of unity and love, that it must be the means of binding hearts together, the cause of life and illumination. If religion becomes the cause of enmity and bloodshed, then irreligion is to be preferred, for religion is the remedy for every ailment, and if a remedy should become the cause of ailment and difficulty, it is better to abandon it. Today in Persia you will see the Muslims, Christians, Zoroastrians, Buddhists assembled together in the same meeting, living in accordance with the teachings of Bahá'u'lláh, manifesting utmost love and accord. Rancor, hatred, antagonism and violence have disappeared; they live together as one family.

And ye who are the people of the Orient—the Orient which has ever been the dawning point of lights from whence the Sun of Reality has ever shone forth, casting its effulgence upon the West—ye, therefore, must become the manifestations of lights. Ye must become brilliant lamps. Ye must shine as stars radiating the light of love toward all mankind. May you be the cause of love amongst the nations. Thus may the world become witness that the Orient has ever been the dawning point of illumination, the source of love and reconciliation. Make peace with all the world. Love everybody; serve everybody. All are the servants of God. God has created all. He provideth for all. He is kind to all. Therefore, must we be kind to all.

I am greatly pleased with this meeting. I am joyous and happy, for here in these western regions I find Orientals seeking education and who are free from prejudice. May God assist you!

12 OCTOBER 1912

––––––––––––––

TALK AT
TEMPLE EMMANU-EL

450 SUTTER STREET,
SAN FRANCISCO, CALIFORNIA

Notes by Bijou Straun

The greatest bestowal of God in the world of humanity is religion, for assuredly the divine teachings of religion are above all other sources of instruction and development to man. Religion confers upon man eternal life and guides his footsteps in the world of morality. It opens the doors of unending happiness and bestows everlasting honor upon the human kingdom. It has been the basis of all civilization and progress in the history of mankind.

We will, therefore, investigate religion, seeking from an unprejudiced standpoint to discover whether it is the source of illumination, the cause of development and the animating impulse of all human advancement. We will investigate independently, free from the restrictions of dogmatic beliefs, blind imitations of ancestral forms and the influence of mere human opinion; for as we enter this question, we will find some who declare that religion is a cause of uplift and betterment in the world, while others assert just as positively that it is a detriment and a source of degradation to mankind. We must give these questions thorough and impartial consideration so that no doubt or uncertainty may linger in our minds regarding them.

How shall we determine whether religion has been the cause of human advancement or retrogression?

We will first consider the Founders of the religions—the Prophets—review the story of Their lives, compare the conditions preceding Their appearance with those subsequent to Their departure, following historical records and irrefutable facts instead of relying upon traditionary statements which are open to both acceptance and denial.

Among the great Prophets was Abraham, Who, being an iconoclast and a Herald of the oneness of God, was banished from His native land. He founded a family upon which the blessing of God descended, and it was owing to this religious basis and ordination that the Abrahamic house progressed and advanced. Through the divine benediction noteworthy and luminous prophets issued from His lineage. There appeared Isaac, Ishmael, Jacob, Joseph, Moses, Aaron, David and Solomon. The Holy Land was conquered by the power of the Covenant of God with Abraham, and the glory of the Solomonic wisdom and sovereignty dawned. All this was due to the religion of God which this blessed lineage established and upheld. It is evident that throughout the history of Abraham and His posterity this was the source of their honor, advancement and civilization. Even today the descendants of His household and lineage are found throughout the world.

There is another and more significant aspect to this religious impulse and impetus. The children of Israel were in bondage and captivity in the land of Egypt four hundred years. They were in an extreme state of degradation and slavery under the tyranny and oppression of the Egyptians. While they were in the condition of abject poverty, in the lowest degree of abasement, ignorance and servility, Moses suddenly appeared among them. Although He was but a shepherd, such majesty, grandeur and efficiency became manifest in Him through the power of religion that His influence continues to this day. His Prophethood was established throughout the land, and the law of His Word became the foundation of the laws of the nations. This unique Personage, single and alone, rescued the children of Israel from bondage through the power of religious training and discipline. He led them to the Holy Land and founded there a great civilization which has become permanent and renowned and under which these people attained the highest degree of honor and glory. He freed them from bondage and captivity. He imbued them with qualities of progressiveness and capability. They proved to be a civilizing people with instincts toward education and scholastic attainment. Their philosophy became renowned; their industries were celebrated throughout the nations. In all lines of advancement which characterize a progressive people they achieved distinction. In the splendor of the reign of Solomon their sciences and arts advanced to such a degree that even the Greek philosophers journeyed to Jerusalem to sit at the feet of the Hebrew sages and acquire the basis of Israelitish law. According to eastern history this is an established fact. Even Socrates visited the Jewish doctors in the Holy Land, consorting with them and discussing the principles and basis of their religious belief. After his return to Greece he formulated his philosophical teaching of divine unity and advanced his belief in the immortality of the spirit beyond the dissolution of the body. Without doubt, Socrates absorbed these verities from the wise men of the Jews with whom he came in contact. Hippocrates and other philosophers of the Greeks likewise visited Palestine and acquired wisdom from the Jewish prophets, studying the basis of ethics and morality, returning to their country with contributions which have made Greece famous.

When a movement fundamentally religious makes a weak nation strong, changes a nondescript tribal people into a mighty and powerful civilization, rescues them from captivity and elevates them to sovereignty, transforms their ignorance into knowledge and endows them with an impetus of advancement in all degrees of development (this is not theory, but historical fact), it becomes evident that religion is the cause of man's attainment to honor and sublimity.

But when we speak of religion, we mean the essential foundation or reality of religion, not the dogmas and blind imitations which have gradually encrusted it and which are the cause of the decline and effacement of a nation. These are inevitably destructive and a menace and hindrance to a nation's life—even as it is recorded in the Torah and confirmed in history that when the Jews became fettered by empty forms and imitations, the wrath of God became manifest. When they forsook the foundations of the law of God, Nebuchadnezzar came and conquered the Holy Land. He killed and made captive the people of Israel, laid waste the country and populous cities and burned the villages. Seventy thousand Jews were carried away captive to Babylon. He destroyed Jerusalem, despoiled the great Temple, desecrated the Holy of Holies and burned the Torah, the heavenly book of Scriptures. Therefore, we learn that allegiance to the essential foundation of the divine religions is ever the cause of development and progress, whereas the abandonment and beclouding of that essential reality through blind imitations and adherence to dogmatic beliefs are the causes of a nation's debasement and degradation. After their conquest by the Babylonians the Jews were successively subjugated by the Greeks and Romans. Under the Roman general Titus in A.D. 70 the Holy Land was stripped and pillaged, Jerusalem razed to its foundations and the Israelites scattered broadcast throughout the world. So complete was their dispersion that they have continued without a country and government of their own to the present day.

From this review of the history of the Jewish people we learn that the foundation of the religion of God laid by Moses was the cause of their eternal honor and national prestige, the animating impulse of their advancement and racial supremacy and the source of that excellence which will always command the respect and reverence of those who understand their peculiar destiny and outcome. The dogmas and blind imitations which gradually obscured the reality of the religion of God proved to be Israel's destructive influences, causing the expulsion of these chosen people from the Holy Land of their Covenant and promise.

What, then, is the mission of the divine Prophets? Their mission is the education and advancement of the world of humanity. They are the real Teachers and Educators, the universal Instructors of mankind. If we wish to discover whether any one of these great Souls or Messengers was in reality a Prophet of God, we must investigate the facts surrounding His life and history, and the first point of our investigation will be the education He bestowed upon mankind. If He has been an Educator, if He has really trained a nation or people, causing it to rise from the lowest depths of ignorance to the highest station of knowledge, then we are sure that He was a Prophet. This is a plain and clear method of procedure, proof that is irrefutable. We do not need to seek after other proofs. We do not need to mention miracles, saying that out of rock water gushed forth, for such miracles and statements may be denied and refused by those who hear them. The deeds of Moses are conclusive evidences of His Prophethood. If a man be fair, unbiased and willing to investigate reality, he will undoubtedly testify to the fact that Moses was, verily, a man of God and a great Personage.

In further consideration of this subject, I wish you to be fair and reasonable in your judgment, setting aside all religious prejudices. We should earnestly seek and thoroughly investigate realities, recognizing that the purpose of the religion of God is the education of humanity and the unity and fellowship of mankind. Furthermore, we will establish the point that the foundations of the religions of God are one foundation. This foundation is not multiple, for it is reality itself. Reality does not admit of multiplicity, although each of the divine religions is separable into two divisions. One concerns the world of morality and the ethical training of human nature. It is directed to the advancement of the world of humanity in general; it reveals and inculcates the knowledge of God and makes possible the discovery of the verities of life. This is ideal and spiritual teaching, the essential quality of divine religion, and not subject to change or transformation. It is the one foundation of all the religions of God. Therefore, the religions are essentially one and the same.

The second classification or division comprises social laws and regulations applicable to human conduct. This is not the essential spiritual quality of religion. It is subject to change and transformation according to the exigencies and requirements of time and place. For instance, in the time of Noah certain requirements made it necessary that all seafood be allowable or lawful. During the time of the Abrahamic Prophethood it was considered allowable, because of a certain exigency, that a man should marry his aunt, even as Sarah was the sister of Abraham's mother. During the cycle of Adam it was lawful and expedient for a man to marry his own sister, even as Abel, Cain and Seth, the sons of Adam, married their sisters. But in the law of the Pentateuch revealed by Moses these marriages were forbidden and their custom and sanction abrogated. Other laws formerly valid were annulled during the time of Moses. For example, it was lawful in Abraham's cycle to eat the flesh of the camel, but during the time of Jacob this was prohibited. Such changes and transformations in the teaching of religion are applicable to the ordinary conditions of life, but they are not important or essential. Moses lived in the wilderness of Sinai where crime necessitated direct punishment. There were no penitentiaries or penalties of imprisonment. Therefore, according to the exigency of the time and place it was a law of God that an eye should be given for an eye and a tooth for a tooth. It would not be practicable to enforce this law at the present time—for instance, to blind a man who accidentally blinded you. In the Torah there are many commands concerning the punishment of a murderer. It would not be allowable or possible to carry out these ordinances today. Human conditions and exigencies are such that even the question of capital punishment—the one penalty which most nations have continued to enforce for murder—is now under discussion by wise men who are debating its advisability. In fact, laws for the ordinary conditions of life are only valid temporarily. The exigencies of the time of Moses justified cutting off a man's hand for theft, but such a penalty is not allowable now. Time changes conditions, and laws change to suit conditions. We must remember that these changing laws are not the essentials; they are the accidentals of religion. The essential ordinances established by a Manifestation of God are spiritual; they concern moralities, the ethical development of man and faith in God. They are ideal and necessarily permanent—expressions of the one foundation and not amenable to change or transformation. Therefore, the fundamental basis of the revealed religion of God is immutable, unchanging throughout the centuries, not subject to the varying conditions of the human world.

Christ ratified and proclaimed the foundation of the law of Moses. Muḥammad and all the Prophets have revoiced that same foundation of reality. Therefore, the purposes and accomplishments of the divine Messengers have been one and the same. They were the source of advancement to the body politic and the cause of the honor and divine civilization of humanity, the foundation of which is one and the same in every dispensation. It is evident, then, that the proofs of the validity and inspiration of a Prophet of God are the deeds of beneficent accomplishment and greatness emanating from Him. If He proves to be instrumental in the elevation and betterment of mankind, He is undoubtedly a valid and heavenly Messenger.

I wish you to be reasonable and just in your consideration of the following statements:

At the time when the Israelites had been dispersed by the power of the Roman Empire and the national life of the Hebrew people had been effaced by their conquerors—when the law of God had seemingly passed from them and the foundation of the religion of God was apparently destroyed—Jesus Christ appeared. When He arose among the Jews, the first thing He did was to proclaim the validity of the Manifestation of Moses. He declared that the Torah, the Old Testament, was the Book of God and that all the prophets of Israel were valid and true. He extolled the mission of Moses, and through His proclamation the name of Moses was spread throughout the world. Through Christianity the greatness of Moses became known among all nations. It is a fact that before the appearance of Christ, the name of Moses had not been heard in Persia. In India they had no knowledge of Judaism, and it was only through the Christianizing of Europe that the teachings of the Old Testament became spread in that region. Throughout Europe there was not a copy of the Old Testament. But consider this carefully and judge it aright: Through the instrumentality of Christ, through the translation of the New Testament, the little volume of the Gospel, the Old Testament, the Torah, has been translated into six hundred languages and spread everywhere in the world. The names of the Hebrew prophets became household words among the nations, who believed that the children of Israel were, verily, the chosen people of God, a holy nation under the especial blessing and protection of God, and that, therefore, the prophets who had arisen in Israel were the daysprings of revelation and brilliant stars in the heaven of the will of God.

Therefore, Christ really promulgated Judaism; for he was a Jew and not opposed to the Jews. He did not deny the Prophethood of Moses; on the contrary, He proclaimed and ratified it. He did not invalidate the Torah; He spread its teachings. That portion of the ordinances of Moses which concerned transactions and unimportant conditions underwent transformation, but the essential teachings of Moses were revoiced and confirmed by Christ without change. He left nothing unfinished or incomplete. Likewise, through the supreme efficacy and power of the Word of God He united most of the nations of the East and the West. This was accomplished at a time when these nations were opposed to each other in hostility and strife. He led them beneath the overshadowing tent of the oneness of humanity. He educated them until they became united and agreed, and through His spirit of conciliation the Roman, Greek, Chaldean and Egyptian were blended in a composite civilization. This wonderful power and extraordinary efficacy of the Word prove conclusively the validity of Christ. Consider how His heavenly sovereignty is still permanent and lasting. Verily, this is conclusive proof and manifest evidence.

From another horizon we see Muḥammad, the Prophet of Arabia, appearing. You may not know that the first address of Muḥammad to His tribe was the statement, "Verily, Moses was a Prophet of God, and the Torah is a Book of God. Verily, O ye people, ye must believe in the Torah, in Moses and the prophets. Ye must accept all the prophets of Israel as valid." In the Qur'án, the Muslim Bible, there are seven statements or repetitions of the Mosaic narrative, and in all the historic accounts Moses is praised. Muḥammad announces that Moses was the greatest Prophet of God, that God guided Him in the wilderness of Sinai, that through the light of guidance Moses hearkened to the summons of God, that He was the Interlocutor of God and the bearer of the tablet of the Ten

Commandments, that all the contemporary nations of the world arose against Him and that eventually Moses conquered them, for falsehood and error are ever overcome by truth. There are many other instances of Muḥammad's confirmation of Moses. I am mentioning but a few. Consider that Muḥammad was born among the savage and barbarous tribes of Arabia, lived among them and was outwardly illiterate and uninformed of the Holy Books of God. The Arabian people were in the utmost ignorance and barbarism. They buried their infant daughters alive, considering this to be an evidence of a valorous and lofty nature. They lived in bondage and serfdom under the Persian and Roman governments and were scattered throughout the desert, engaged in continual strife and bloodshed. When the light of Muḥammad dawned, the darkness of ignorance was dispelled from the deserts of Arabia. In a short period of time those barbarous peoples attained a superlative degree of civilization which, with Baghdád as its center, extended as far westward as Spain and afterward influenced the greater part of Europe. What proof of Prophethood could be greater than this, unless we close our eyes to justice and remain obstinately opposed to reason?

Today the Christians are believers in Moses, accept Him as a Prophet of God and praise Him most highly. The Muslims are, likewise, believers in Moses, accept the validity of His Prophethood, at the same time believing in Christ. Could it be said that the acceptance of Moses by the Christians and Muslims has been harmful and detrimental to those people?

On the contrary, it has been beneficial to them, proving that they have been fair-minded and just. What harm could result to the Jewish people, then, if they in return should accept Christ and acknowledge the validity of the Prophethood of Muḥammad? By this acceptance and praiseworthy attitude the enmity and hatred which have afflicted mankind so many centuries would be dispelled, fanaticism and bloodshed pass away and the world be blessed by unity and agreement. Christians and Muslims believe and admit that Moses was the Interlocutor of God. Why do you not say that Christ was the Word of God? Why do you not speak these few words that will do away with all this difficulty? Then there will be no more hatred and fanaticism, no more warfare and bloodshed in the Land of Promise. Then there will be peace among you forever.

Verily, I now declare to you that Moses was the Interlocutor of God and a most noteworthy Prophet, that Moses revealed the fundamental law of God and founded the real ethical basis of the civilization and progress of humanity. What harm is there in this? Have I lost anything by saying this to you and believing it as a Bahá'í? On the contrary, it benefits me; and Bahá'u'lláh, the Founder of the Bahá'í Movement, confirms me, saying, "You have been fair and just in your judgment; you have impartially investigated the truth and arrived at a true conclusion; you have announced your belief in Moses, a Prophet of God, and accepted the Torah, the Book of God." Inasmuch as it is possible for me to sweep away all evidences of prejudice by such a liberal and universal statement of belief, why is it not possible for you to do likewise? Why not put an end to this religious strife and establish a bond of connection between the hearts of men? Why should not the followers of one religion praise the Founder or Teacher of another? The other religionists extol the greatness of Moses and admit that He was the Founder of Judaism. Why do the Hebrews refuse to praise and accept the other great Messengers Who have appeared in the world? What harm could there be in this? What rightful objection? None whatever. You would lose nothing by such action and statement. On the contrary, you would contribute to the welfare of mankind. You would be instrumental in establishing the happiness of the world of humanity. The eternal honor of man depends upon the liberalism of this modern age. Inasmuch as our God is one God and the Creator of all mankind, He provides for and protects all. We acknowledge Him as a God of kindness, justice and mercy. Why then should we, His children and followers, war and fight, bringing sorrow and grief into the hearts of each other? God is loving and merciful. His intention in religion has ever been the bond of unity and affinity between humankind.

Praise be to God! The medieval ages of darkness have passed away and this century of radiance has dawned, this century wherein the reality of things is becoming evident, wherein science is penetrating the mysteries of the universe, the oneness of the world of humanity is being established, and service to mankind is the paramount motive of all existence.

Shall we remain steeped in our fanaticisms and cling to our prejudices? Is it fitting that we should still be bound and restricted by ancient fables and superstitions of the past, be handicapped by superannuated beliefs and the ignorances of dark ages, waging religious wars, fighting and shedding blood, shunning and anathematizing each other? Is this becoming? Is it not better for us to be loving and considerate toward each other? Is it not preferable to enjoy fellowship and unity, join in anthems of praise to the most high God and extol all His Prophets in the spirit of acceptance and true vision? Then, indeed, this world will become a paradise, and the promised Day of God will dawn. Then, according to the prophecy of Isaiah, the wolf and the lamb will drink from the same stream, the owl and the vulture will nest together in the same branches, and the lion and the calf pasture in the same meadow. What does this mean? It means that fierce and contending religions, hostile creeds and divergent beliefs will reconcile and associate, notwithstanding their former hatreds and antagonism. Through the liberalism of human attitude demanded in this radiant century they will blend together in perfect fellowship and love. This is the spirit and meaning of Isaiah's words. There will never be a day when this prophecy will come to pass literally, for these animals by their natures cannot mingle and associate in kindness and love. Therefore, this prophecy symbolizes the unity and agreement of races, nations and peoples who will come together in attitudes of intelligence, illumination and spirituality.

The age has dawned when human fellowship will become a reality.

The century has come when all religions shall be unified.

The dispensation is at hand when all nations shall enjoy the blessings of international peace.

The cycle has arrived when racial prejudice will be abandoned by tribes and peoples of the world.

The epoch has begun wherein all native lands will be conjoined in one great human family.

For all mankind shall dwell in peace and security beneath the shelter of the great tabernacle of the one living God.

25 OCTOBER 1912

TALK AT
HOTEL SACRAMENTO

SACRAMENTO, CALIFORNIA

Notes by Bijou Straun

When Christ appeared, certain blessed souls followed His example. They were with their Master, ever watching and observing His conduct, movements and thoughts. They witnessed the persecutions which were heaped upon Him and were informed of all the events appertaining to that marvelous life—recipients of His kindness and favors. After the ascension of Christ they hastened to various regions of the world, scattering broadcast the teachings and instructions which He had given them. Through their devotion and efforts other places and remote nations became informed of the principles revealed by Him.

Through their instrumentality the East was illumined, and the light which flooded the East flooded the West. This light was the cause of guiding great hosts of people. It proved to be a preventive of warfare in many instances. This is evidenced in the unification and conjoining of various nations which had formerly been hostile to each other—such as the Greeks, Romans, Egyptians, Syrians, Chaldeans and Assyrians. Through Christ the oneness of the world of humanity received its expression and proved to be the cause of spiritual illumination for mankind. The breaths of the Holy Spirit became effective in the hearts of people.

Now we have, likewise, come from the Orient, announcing the appearance of Bahá'u'lláh, Who shone from the horizon of the East. We have observed His life and beheld His deeds. We have been witnesses of His ordeals and sufferings, observers of His imprisonment and exile. We are fully acquainted with the persecutions heaped upon His blessed Personality. Therefore, we who are His disciples have been scattered throughout the world in order that His teachings may be widespread and be heard by every ear. Thus may the people receive the glad tidings of the dawn of His great dispensation, become aware of the divine evidences manifest in Him, be informed of the wonderful episodes of His marvelous life, the greatness of His power in withstanding the kings of the Orient, the might of His spirit in upholding under all circumstances the standard of the oneness of the world of mankind. Perchance you have heard or read of Him. I will give you a brief epitome of His life in order that you may be informed of the history of His great movement and know His teachings.

Bahá'u'lláh was a Persian personage descended from prominent lineage. During His early years a Youth Whose name was 'Alí-Muḥammad appeared in Persia. He was entitled the Báb, which means door or gate. The bearer of this title was a great Soul from Whom spiritual signs and evidences became manifest. He withstood the tests of time and lived contrary to the custom and usages of Persia. He revealed a new system of faith opposed to the beliefs in His country and promulgated certain principles contrary to the thoughts of the people. For this, that remarkable Personality was imprisoned by the Persian government. Eventually, by order of the government He was martyred. The account of this martyrdom, briefly stated, is as follows: He was suspended in a square as a target and shot to death. This revered Personage foreshadowed the advent of another Soul of Whom He said, "When He cometh He shall reveal greater things unto you."

Thus, after the martyrdom of the Báb, Bahá'u'lláh appeared. The government arose against Him. The priesthood in Persia opposed Him, subjecting Him to severe persecution. His possessions were confiscated, His relatives and friends were killed, and He was placed in a dungeon. For a long period He was imprisoned, chained and subjected to severest suffering. Afterward, He was exiled to 'Iráq, or Mesopotamia, from thence to Constantinople, then transferred to Adrianople and finally to 'Akká in Syria. He spent twenty-four years in the prison of 'Akká, where He underwent the severest ordeals and privations without a day or night of relaxation and repose. Notwithstanding this imprisonment and suffering, He manifested utmost spiritual power and majesty. Although imprisoned, He withstood two tyrant kings and eventually overcame both.

Shortly after His imprisonment He addressed Epistles, or Tablets, to all the kings and rulers of the world, summoning them to universal peace, to unity and international brotherhood. Among these sovereigns was the Sháh of Persia, through whose instrumentality chiefly He had been imprisoned. In His letter to that ruler He arraigned him severely and prophesied his downfall, saying, "Thou art a tyrant; thy country will be laid waste; and thy family, humiliated and debased." He wrote to the Sulṭán of Turkey in similar terms, saying, "Thy dominion will pass away from thee." The Epistles to the kings and rulers summoning them to international peace were written by Bahá'u'lláh fifty years ago. Everything He wrote has come to pass. These letters were published in Bombay thirty years ago and are now spread broadcast throughout the world. Briefly, Bahá'u'lláh endured forty years of vicissitudes, ordeals and hardships for the purpose of spreading His teachings, which may be mentioned as follows:

The first teaching is that man should investigate reality, for reality is contrary to dogmatic interpretations and imitations of ancestral forms of belief to which all nations and peoples adhere so tenaciously. These blind imitations are contrary to the fundamental basis of the divine religions, for the divine religions in their central and essential teaching are based upon unity, love and peace, whereas these variations and imitations have ever been productive of warfare, sedition and strife. Therefore, all souls should consider it incumbent upon them to investigate reality. Reality is one; and when found, it will unify all mankind. Reality is the love of God. Reality is the knowledge of God. Reality is justice. Reality is the oneness or solidarity of mankind. Reality is international peace. Reality is the knowledge of verities. Reality unifies humanity.

In brief, His theme was that reality underlies all the great religious systems of the world. He summoned the nations and peoples of the world to it. Hostile nations because of their acceptance of the reality of His words became unified. Strife, discord and contention among them passed away; they attained a station of utmost love. At present in Asia those who have accepted His teachings and followed His example, although formerly most hostile and bitter toward each other, now associate in brotherhood and fellowship. The strife and warfare of past times have ceased among them. Jews, Zoroastrians, Christians, Muslims and others have attained to a superlative state of love and agreement through Bahá'u'lláh. They now consort together as one family. They have investigated reality. Reality does not accept multiplicity, nor is it subject to divisibility. These irreconcilable peoples have become unified and agreed.

The second teaching of Bahá'u'lláh is the principle of the oneness of the world of humanity. God is one; His servants are, likewise, one. God has created all; He is kind to all. Inasmuch as He is such a tender Father to all, why should His children disagree? Why should they war and fight? Like the Heavenly Father we must live in love and unity. Man is the temple of God, the image and likeness of the Lord. Surely if one should destroy the temple of God, he will incur the displeasure of the Creator. For this reason, we must live together in amity and love. Bahá'u'lláh has addressed the world of humanity, saying, "Verily, ye are the fruits of one tree and the leaves of one branch." This signifies that the entire world of humanity is one tree. The various nations and peoples are the branches of that tree. Individual members of mankind are represented by the twigs and blossoms. Why should these parts of the same tree manifest strife and discord toward each other?

The third teaching of Bahá'u'lláh concerns universal peace among the nations, among the religions, among the races and native lands. He has declared that so long as prejudice—whether religious, racial, patriotic, political or sectarian—continues to exist among mankind, universal peace cannot become a reality in the world. From the earliest history of man down to the present time all the wars and bloodshed which have taken place were caused either by religious, racial, political or sectarian bias. Therefore, it is evident that so long as these prejudices continue, the world of humanity cannot attain peace and composure.

Among the teachings of Bahá'u'lláh is His declaration that religion must be the cause of love and fellowship, must be the source of unity in the hearts of men. If religion becomes a cause of enmity and hatred, it is evident that the abolition of religion is preferable to its promulgation; for religion is a remedy for human ills. If a remedy should be productive of disease, it is certainly advisable to abandon it.

Furthermore, the teachings of Bahá'u'lláh announce that religion must be in conformity with science and reason; otherwise, it is superstition; for science and reason are realities, and religion itself is the Divine Reality unto which true science and reason must conform. God has bestowed the gift of mind upon man in order that he may weigh every fact or truth presented to him and adjudge whether it be reasonable. That which conforms to his reason he may accept as true, while that which reason and science cannot sanction may be discarded as imagination and superstition, as a phantom and not reality. Inasmuch as the blind imitations or dogmatic interpretations current among men do not coincide with the postulates of reason, and the mind and scientific investigation cannot acquiesce thereto, many souls in the human world today shun and deny religion. That is to say, imitations, when weighed in the scales of reason, will not conform to its standard and requirement. Therefore, these souls deny religion and become irreligious, whereas if the reality of the divine religions becomes manifest to them and the foundation of the heavenly teachings is revealed coinciding with facts and evident truths, reconciling with scientific knowledge and reasonable proof, all may acknowledge them, and irreligion will cease to exist. In this way all mankind may be brought to the foundation of religion, for reality is true reason and science, while all that is not conformable thereto is mere superstition.

The teachings of Bahá'u'lláh also proclaim equality between man and woman, for He has declared that all are the servants of God and endowed with capacity for the attainment of virtues and bestowals. All are the manifestations of the mercy of the Lord. In the creation of God no distinction obtains. All are His servants. In the estimation of God there is no gender. The one whose deeds are more worthy, whose sayings are better, whose accomplishments are more useful is nearest and dearest in the estimation of God, be that one male or female. When we look upon creation, we find the male and female principle apparent in all phenomena of existence. In the vegetable kingdom we find the male and female fig tree, the male and female palm, the mulberry tree and so on. All plant life is characterized by this difference in gender, but no distinction or preference is evidenced. Nay, rather, there is perfect equality. Likewise, in the animal kingdom gender obtains; we have male and female, but no distinction or preference. Perfect equality is manifest. The animal, bereft of the degree of human reason and comprehension, is unable to appreciate the questions of suffrage, nor does it assert its prerogative. Man, endowed with his higher reason, accomplished in attainments and comprehending the realities of things, will surely not be willing to allow a great part of humanity to remain defective or deprived. This would be the utmost injustice. The world of humanity is possessed of two wings: the male and the female. So long as these two wings are not equivalent in strength, the bird will not fly. Until womankind reaches the same degree as man, until she enjoys the same arena of activity, extraordinary attainment for humanity will not be realized; humanity cannot wing its way to heights of real attainment. When the two wings or parts become equivalent in strength, enjoying the same prerogatives, the flight of man will be exceedingly lofty and extraordinary. Therefore, woman must receive the same education as man and all inequality be adjusted. Thus, imbued with the same virtues as man, rising through all the degrees of human attainment, women will become the peers of men, and until this equality is established, true progress and attainment for the human race will not be facilitated.

The evident reasons underlying this are as follows: Woman by nature is opposed to war; she is an advocate of peace. Children are reared and brought up by the mothers who give them the first principles of education and labor assiduously in their behalf. Consider, for instance, a mother who has tenderly reared a son for twenty years to the age of maturity. Surely she will not consent to having that son torn asunder and killed in the field of battle. Therefore, as woman advances toward the degree of man in power and privilege, with the right of vote and control in human government, most assuredly war will cease; for woman is naturally the most devoted and staunch advocate of international peace.

Bahá'u'lláh teaches that material civilization is incomplete, insufficient and that divine civilization must be established. Material civilization concerns the world of matter or bodies, but divine civilization is the realm of ethics and moralities. Until the moral degree of the nations is advanced and human virtues attain a lofty level, happiness for mankind is impossible. The philosophers have founded material civilization. The Prophets have founded divine civilization. Christ was the Founder of heavenly civilization. Mankind receives the bounties of material civilization as well as divine civilization from the heavenly Prophets. The capacity for achieving extraordinary and praiseworthy progress is bestowed by Them through the breaths of the Holy Spirit, and heavenly civilization is not possible of attainment or accomplishment otherwise. This evidences the need of humanity for heavenly bestowals, and until these heavenly bestowals are received, eternal happiness cannot be realized.

In brief, the purport is this: The teachings of Bahá'u'lláh are boundless, innumerable; time will not allow us to mention them in detail. The foundation of progress and real prosperity in the human world is reality, for reality is the divine standard and the bestowal of God. Reality is reasonableness, and reasonableness is ever conducive to the honorable station of man. Reality is the guidance of God. Reality is the cause of illumination of mankind. Reality is love, ever working for the welfare of humanity. Reality is the bond which conjoins hearts. This ever uplifts man toward higher stages of progress and attainment. Reality is the unity of mankind, conferring everlasting life. Reality is perfect equality, the foundation of agreement between the nations, the first step toward international peace.

8 NOVEMBER 1912

———————————

TALK AT EIGHTH STREET TEMPLE, SYNAGOGUE

———————————

WASHINGTON, D. C.

Notes by Joseph H. Hannen

God is one, the effulgence of God is one, and humanity constitutes the servants of that one God. God is kind to all. He creates and provides for all, and all are under His care and protection. The Sun of Truth, the Word of God, shines upon all mankind; the divine cloud pours down its precious rain; the gentle zephyrs of His mercy blow, and all humanity is submerged in the ocean of His eternal justice and loving-kindness. God has created mankind from the same progeny in order that they may associate in good fellowship, exercise love toward each other and live together in unity and brotherhood.

But we have acted contrary to the will and good pleasure of God. We have been the cause of enmity and disunion. We have separated from each other and risen against each other in opposition and strife. How many have been the wars between peoples and nations! What bloodshed! Numberless are the cities and homes which have been laid waste. All of this has been contrary to the good pleasure of God, for He hath willed love for humanity. He is clement and merciful to all His creatures. He hath ordained amity and fellowship amongst men.

Most regrettable of all is the state of difference and divergence we have created between each other in the name of religion, imagining that a paramount duty in our religious belief is that of alienation and estrangement, that we should shun each other and consider each other contaminated with error and infidelity. In reality, the foundations of the divine religions are one and the same. The differences which have arisen between us are due to blind imitations of dogmatic beliefs and adherence to ancestral forms of worship. Abraham was the founder of reality. Moses, Christ, Muḥammad were the manifestations of reality. Bahá'-u'lláh was the glory of reality. This is not simply an assertion; it will be proved.

Let me ask your closest attention in considering this subject. The divine religions embody two kinds of ordinances. First, there are those which constitute essential, or spiritual, teachings of the Word of God. These are faith in God, the acquirement of the virtues which characterize perfect manhood, praiseworthy moralities, the acquisition of the bestowals and bounties emanating from the divine effulgences—in brief, the ordinances which concern the realm of morals and ethics. This is the fundamental aspect of the religion of God, and this is of the highest importance because knowledge of God is the fundamental requirement of man. Man must comprehend the oneness of Divinity. He must come to know and acknowledge the precepts of God and realize for a certainty that the ethical development of humanity is dependent upon religion. He must get rid of all defects and seek the attainment of heavenly virtues in order that he may prove to be the image and likeness of God. It is recorded in the Holy Bible that God said, "Let us make

man in our image, after our likeness." It is self-evident
that the image and likeness mentioned do not apply
to the form and semblance of a human being because
the reality of Divinity is not limited to any form or
figure. Nay, rather, the attributes and characteristics
of God are intended. Even as God is pronounced to
be just, man must likewise be just. As God is loving
and kind to all men, man must likewise manifest
loving-kindness to all humanity. As God is loyal and
truthful, man must show forth the same attributes in
the human world. Even as God exercises mercy toward all, man must prove himself to be the manifestation of mercy. In a word, the image and likeness of
God constitute the virtues of God, and man is intended to become the recipient of the effulgences of
divine attributes. This is the essential foundation of
all the divine religions, the reality itself, common to
all. Abraham promulgated this; Moses proclaimed it.
Christ and all the Prophets upheld this standard and
aspect of divine religion.

Second, there are laws and ordinances which are
temporary and nonessential. These concern human
transactions and relations. They are accidental and
subject to change according to the exigencies of time
and place. These ordinances are neither permanent
nor fundamental. For instance, during the time of
Noah it was expedient that seafood be considered as
lawful; therefore, God commanded Noah to partake
of all marine animal life. During the time of Moses
this was not in accordance with the exigencies of Israel's existence; therefore, a second command was re-

vealed partly abrogating the law concerning marine foods. During the time of Abraham—upon Him be peace!—camel's milk was considered a lawful and acceptable food; likewise, the flesh of the camel; but during Jacob's time, because of a certain vow He made, this became unlawful. These are nonessential, temporary laws. In the Holy Bible there are certain commandments which according to those bygone times constituted the very spirit of the age, the very light of that period. For example, according to the law of the Torah if a man committed theft of a certain amount, they cut off his hand. Is it practicable and reasonable in this present day to cut off a man's hand for the theft of a dollar? In the Torah there are ten ordinances concerning murder. Could these be made effective today? Unquestionably no; times have changed. According to the explicit text of the Bible if a man should change or break the law of the Sabbath or if he should touch fire on the Sabbath, he must be killed. Today such a law is abrogated. The Torah declares that if a man should speak a disrespectful word to his father, he should suffer the penalty of death. Is this possible of enforcement now? No; human conditions have undergone changes. Likewise, during the time of Christ certain minor ordinances conformable to that period were enforced.

It has been shown conclusively, therefore, that the foundation of the religion of God remains permanent and unchanging. It is that fixed foundation which ensures the progress and stability of the body politic and the illumination of humanity. It has ever been the cause of love and justice amongst men. It works for the true fellowship and unification of all mankind, for it never changes and is not subject to supersedure. The accidental, or nonessential, laws which regulate the transactions of the social body and everyday affairs of life are changeable and subject to abrogation.

Let me ask: What is the purpose of Prophethood? Why has God sent the Prophets? It is self-evident that the Prophets are the Educators of men and the Teachers of the human race. They come to bestow universal education upon humanity, to give humanity training, to uplift the human race from the abyss of despair and desolation and to enable man to attain the apogee of advancement and glory. The people are in darkness; the Prophets bring them into the realm of light. They are in a state of utter imperfection; the Prophets imbue them with perfections. The purpose of the prophetic mission is none other than the education and guidance of the people. Therefore, we must regard and be on the lookout for the man who is thus qualified—that is to say, any soul who proves to be the Educator of mankind and the Teacher of the human race is undoubtedly the Prophet of His age.

For example, let us review the events connected with the history of Moses—upon Him be peace! He dwelt in Midian at a time when the children of Israel were in captivity and bondage in the land of Egypt, subjected to every tyranny and severe oppression. They were illiterate and ignorant, undergoing cruel ordeals and experiences. They were in such a state of helplessness and impotence that it was proverbial to state that one Egyptian could overcome ten Israelites. At such a time as this and under such forbidding conditions Moses appeared and shone forth with a heavenly radiance. He saved Israel from the bondage of Pharaoh and released them from captivity. He led them out of the land of Egypt and into the Holy Land. They had been scattered and broken; He unified and disciplined them, conferred upon them the blessing of wisdom and knowledge. They had been slaves; He made them princes. They were ignorant; He made them learned. They were imperfect; He enabled them to attain perfection. In a word, He led them out of their condition of hopelessness and brought them to efficiency in the plane of confidence and valor. They became renowned throughout the ancient world until finally in the zenith and splendor of their new civilization the glory of the sovereignty of Solomon was attained. Through the guidance and training of Moses these slaves and captives became the dominating people amongst the nations. Not only in physical and military superiority were they renowned, but in all the degrees of arts, letters and refinement their fame was widespread. Even the celebrated philosophers of Greece journeyed to Jerusalem in order to study with the Israelitish sages, and many were the lessons of philosophy and wisdom they received. Among these philosophers was the famous Socrates. He visited the Holy Land and studied with the prophets of Israel, acquiring principles of their philosophical teaching and a knowledge of their advanced arts and sciences. After his return to Greece he founded the system known as the unity of God. The Greek people rose against him, and at last he was poisoned in the presence of the king. Hippocrates and many other Greek philosophers sat at the feet of the learned Israelitish doctors and absorbed their expositions of wisdom and inner truth.

Inasmuch as Moses through the influence of His great mission was instrumental in releasing the Israelites from a low state of debasement and humiliation, establishing them in a station of prestige and glorification, disciplining and educating them, it is necessary for us to reach a fair and just judgment in regard to such a marvelous Teacher. For in this great accomplishment He stood single and alone. Could He have made such a change and brought about such a condition among these people without the sanction and assistance of a heavenly power? Could He have transformed a people from humiliation to glory without a holy and divine support?

None other than a divine power could have done this. Therein lies the proof of Prophethood because the mission of a Prophet is education of the human race such as this Personage accomplished, proving Him to be a mighty Prophet among the Prophets and His Book the very Book of God. This is a rational, direct and perfect proof.

In brief, Moses—upon Whom be peace!—founded the law of God, purified the morals of the people of Israel and gave them an impetus toward nobler and higher attainments. But after the departure of Moses, following the decline of the glory of Solomon's era and during the reign of Jeroboam there came a great change in this nation. The high ethical standards and spiritual perfections ceased to exist. Conditions and morals became corrupt, religion was debased, and the perfect principles of the Mosaic law were obscured in superstition and polytheism. War and strife arose among the tribes, and their unity was destroyed. The followers of Jeroboam declared themselves rightful and valid in kingly succession, and the supporters of Rehoboam made the same claim. Finally, the tribes were torn asunder by hostility and hatred, the glory of Israel was eclipsed, and so complete was the degradation that a golden calf was set up as an object of worship in the city of Tyre. Thereupon God sent Elijah, the prophet, who redeemed the people, renewed the law of God and established an era of new life for Israel. History shows a still later change and transformation when this oneness and solidarity were followed by another dispersion of the tribes. Nebuchadnezzar, King of Babylon, invaded the Holy Land and carried away captive seventy thousand Israelites to Chaldea, where the greatest reverses, trials and suffering afflicted these unfortunate people. Then the prophets of God again reformed and reestablished the law of God, and the people in their humiliation again followed it. This resulted in their liberation, and under the edict of Cyrus, King of Persia, there was a return to the Holy City. Jerusalem and the Temple of Solomon were rebuilt, and the glory of Israel was restored. This lasted but a short time; the morality of the people declined, and conditions reached an extreme degree until the Roman general Titus took Jerusalem and razed it to its foundations. Pillage and conquest completed the desolation; Palestine became a waste and wilderness, and the Jews fled from the Holy Land of their ancestors. The cause of this disintegration and dispersion was the departure of Israel from the foundation of the law of God revealed by Moses—namely, the acquisition of divine virtues, morality, love, the development of arts and sciences and the spirit of the oneness of humanity.

I now wish you to examine certain facts and statements which are worthy of consideration. My purpose and intention is to remove from the hearts of men the religious enmity and hatred which have fettered them and to bring all religions into agreement and unity. Inasmuch as this hatred and enmity, this bigotry and intolerance are outcomes of misunderstandings, the reality of religious unity will appear when these misunderstandings are dispelled. For the foundation of the divine religions is one foundation. This is the oneness of revelation or teaching. But, alas, we have turned away from that foundation, holding tenaciously to various dogmatic forms and blind imitation of ancestral beliefs. This is the real cause of enmity, hatred and bloodshed in the world—the reason of alienation and estrangement among mankind. Therefore, I wish you to be very just and fair in your judgment of the following statements.

During the time that the people of Israel were being tossed and afflicted by the conditions I have named, Jesus Christ appeared among them. Jesus of

Nazareth was a Jew. He was single and unaided, alone and unique. He had no assistant. The Jews at once pronounced Him to be an enemy of Moses. They declared that He was the destroyer of the Mosaic laws and ordinances. Let us examine the facts as they are, investigate the truth and reality in order to arrive at a true opinion and conclusion. For a completely fair opinion upon this question we must lay aside all we have and investigate independently. This Personage, Jesus Christ, declared Moses to have been the Prophet of God and pronounced all the prophets of Israel as sent from God. He proclaimed the Torah the very Book of God, summoned all to conform to its precepts and follow its teachings. It is an historical fact that during a period of fifteen hundred years the kings of Israel were unable to promulgate broadcast the religion of Judaism. In fact, during that period the name and history of Moses were confined to the boundaries of Palestine and the Torah was a book well known only in that country. But through Christ, through the blessing of the New Testament of Jesus Christ, the Old Testament, the Torah, was translated into six hundred different tongues and spread throughout the world. It was through Christianity that the Torah reached Persia. Before that time there was no knowledge in that country of such a book, but Christ caused its spread and acceptance. Through Him the name of Moses was elevated and revered. He was instrumental in publishing the name and greatness of the Israelitish prophets, and He proved to the world that the Israelites constituted the people of God.

Which of the kings of Israel could have accomplished this? Were it not for Jesus Christ, would the Bible, the Torah have reached this land of America? Would the name of Moses be spread throughout the world? Refer to history. Everyone knows that when Christianity was spread, there was a simultaneous spread of the knowledge of Judaism and the Torah. Throughout the length and breadth of Persia there was not a single volume of the Old Testament until the religion of Jesus Christ caused it to appear everywhere so that today the Holy Bible is a household book in that country. It is evident, then, that Christ was a friend of Moses, that He loved and believed in Moses; otherwise, He would not have commemorated His name and Prophethood. This is self-evident. Therefore, Christians and Jews should have the greatest love for each other because the Founders of these two great religions have been in perfect agreement in Book and teaching. Their followers should be likewise.

We have already stated the valid proofs of Prophethood. We find the very evidences of the validity of Moses were witnessed and duplicated in Christ. Christ was also a unique and single Personage born of the lineage of Israel. By the power of His Word He was able to unite people of the Roman, Greek, Chaldean, Egyptian and Assyrian nations. Whereas they had been cruel, bloodthirsty and hostile, killing, pillaging and taking each other captive, He cemented them together in a perfect bond of unity and love. He caused them to agree and become reconciled. Such mighty effects were the results of the manifestation of one single

Soul. This proves conclusively that Christ was assisted by God. Today all Christians admit and believe that Moses was a Prophet of God. They declare that His Book was the Book of God, that the prophets of Israel were true and valid and that the people of Israel constituted the people of God. What harm has come from this? What harm could come from a statement by the Jews that Jesus was also a Manifestation of the Word of God? Have the Christians suffered for their belief in Moses? Have they experienced any loss of religious enthusiasm or witnessed any defeat in their religious belief by declaring that Moses was a Prophet of God, that the Torah was a Book of God and that all the prophets of Israel were prophets of God? It is evident that no loss comes from this. And now it is time for the Jews to declare that Christ was the Word of God, and then this enmity between two great religions will pass away. For two thousand years this enmity and religious prejudice have continued. Blood has been shed, ordeals have been suffered. These few words will remedy the difficulty and unite two great religions. What harm could follow this: that just as the Christians glorify and praise the name of Moses, likewise the Jews should commemorate the name of Christ, declare Him to be the Word of God and consider Him as one of the chosen Messengers of God?

A few words concerning the Qur'án and the Muslims: When Muḥammad appeared, He spoke of Moses as the great Man of God. In the Qur'án He refers to the sayings of Moses in seven different places, proclaims Him a Prophet and the possessor of a Book, the Founder of the law and the Spirit of God. He said, "Whosoever believes in Him is acceptable in the estimation of God, and whosoever shuns Him or any of the prophets is rejected of God." Even in conclusion He calls upon His own relatives, saying, "Why have ye shunned and not believed in Moses? Why have ye not acknowledged the Torah? Why have ye not believed in the Jewish prophets?" In a certain súrih of the Qur'án He mentions the names of twenty-eight of the prophets of Israel, praising each and all of them. To this great extent He has ratified and commended the prophets and religion of Israel. The purport is this: that Muḥammad praised and glorified Moses and confirmed Judaism. He declared that whosoever denies Moses is contaminated and even if he repents, his repentance will not be accepted. He pronounced His own relatives infidels and impure because they had denied the prophets. He said, "Because you have not believed in Christ, because you have not believed in Moses, because you have not believed in the Gospels, you are infidels and contaminated." In this way Muḥammad has praised the Torah, Moses, Christ and the prophets of the past. He appeared amongst the Arabs, who were a people nomadic and illiterate, barbarous in nature and bloodthirsty. He guided and trained them until they attained a high degree of development. Through His education and discipline they rose from the lowest levels of ignorance to the heights of knowledge, becoming masters of erudition and philosophy. We see, therefore that the proofs applicable to one Prophet are equally applicable to another.

In conclusion, since the Prophets themselves, the Founders, have loved, praised and testified of each other, why should we disagree and be alienated? God is one. He is the Shepherd of all. We are His sheep and, therefore, should live together in love and unity. We should manifest the spirit of justness and goodwill toward each other. Shall we do this, or shall we censure and pronounce anathema, praising ourselves and condemning all others? What possible good can come from such attitude and action? On the contrary, nothing but enmity and hatred, injustice and inhumanity can possibly result. Has not this been the greatest cause of bloodshed, woe and tribulation in the past?

Praise be to God! You are living in a land of freedom. You are blessed with men of learning, men who are well versed in the comparative study of religions. You realize the need of unity and know the great harm which comes from prejudice and superstition. I ask you, is not fellowship and brotherhood preferable to enmity and hatred in society and community? The answer is self-evident. Love and fellowship are absolutely needful to win the good pleasure of God, which is the goal of all human attainment. We must be united. We must love each other. We must ever praise each other. We must bestow commendation upon all people, thus removing the discord and hatred which have caused alienation amongst men. Otherwise, the conditions of the past will continue, praising ourselves and condemning others; religious wars will have no end, and religious prejudice, the prime cause of this havoc and tribulation, will increase. This must be abandoned, and the way to do it is to investigate the reality which underlies all the religions. This underlying reality is the love of humanity. For God is one and humanity is one, and the only creed of the Prophets is love and unity.

9 November 1912

TALK AT HOME OF MR. AND MRS. ARTHUR J. PARSONS

1700 Eighteenth Street, NW,
Washington, D. C.

Notes by Joseph H. Hannen

The address delivered last evening in the Jewish synagogue evidently disturbed some of the people, including the revered rabbi who called upon me this afternoon. Together we went over the ground again, which I shall now review for your benefit.

It was not possible to make the subject completely plain to the rabbi last night, as he was very much pressed for time, but today the opportunity was sufficient for a reconsideration of the statements in detail. I wish you to understand them thoroughly and memorize them in order that you may discourse with the Jews and thus, perchance, become instrumental in leading them aright.

The quintessence of our subject was this: What is the mission of the Prophet, and what is the object of a divine law? In answer we stated: There is no doubt that the purpose of a divine law is the education of the human race, the training of humanity. All mankind may be considered as pupils or children who are in need of a divine Educator, a real Teacher. The essential requirement and qualification of Prophethood is the training and guidance of the people. Therefore, we shall first consider the efficacy of the teachings of those who have been followed and accepted as the Prophets of God. The question that must be answered is: Have They taught mankind? Have They proved Themselves efficient Educators?

Among Them was Moses. We find that He appeared as the leader of the children of Israel during a period of their captivity. They were in a state of extreme humiliation, ignorance and heedlessness, living in a very lowly manner in Egypt under conditions of life worse than death. Imagine an ignorant people, downtrodden and oppressed, thoughtless, negligent and mentally darkened, held in subjection as slaves. Moses was appointed for their deliverance and training. He guided them, led them out of bondage into the Holy Land, uplifted them from ignorance and despair, trained them so that they rose from a condition of lowliness and subjection into one of honor and importance, and enabled them to reach a high degree of perfection. They became proficient in sciences and arts, attained a lofty plane of civilization, honorable and esteemed among nations, whereas formerly they had been lowly and despised. They were ignorant; they became intelligent, finally reaching that period of supremacy and power witnessed in the Solomonic sovereignty. Their name became widespread throughout the world, and they were esteemed for distinct virtues. Even the philosophers of Greece went to Palestine to drink from the fountains of their wisdom and sit at the feet of their sages. All these facts prove that Moses was a Prophet and a Teacher.

As to Christ: He was a single, unique and lowly individual Who appeared at a time when the Israelitish nation had fallen from the heights of its glory to the lowest condition of bondage and contempt, subject to the tyranny of the Roman Empire, living under a yoke of humiliation, ignorant and negligent of God. The historical records of the Holy Books confirm these statements. Christ—this single and unique Personage—appeared amongst these despised and degraded people, reflecting a divine power and the potency of the Holy Spirit. He unified the various peoples and nations of the world, brought them together in fellowship and agreement and gathered them beneath the overshadowing protection of one Word. His prestige and mention were not confined to the children of Israel alone, who were at that time a limited race and people, but His spiritual power had also permeated and united great influential nations who had been warlike and hostile, such as the Romans, Greeks, Egyptians, Chaldeans, Syrians and Assyrians. He dispelled their hostility, healed their hatred, made them a united people, and by His Word created the utmost love amongst them so that they advanced immeasurably in the degrees of education and human perfection, thereby attaining a never-ending glory.

The Jews had become dispersed and widely scattered. This single and unique Personage overcame all the then known world, founding an everlasting sovereignty, a mighty nation indeed. Such a result proved Him to be a great man, the first Educator of His time, the first Teacher of His period. What proofs could be greater than these? What would be more convincing than this evidence that a single individual resuscitated so many nations and peoples, unified so many tribes and sects, removed so much warfare and hatred? Undoubtedly, such accomplishment could be wrought only through the power of God and not by mere human effort, which is altogether incapable of producing these mighty results.

When Christ appeared, the Jews pronounced Him an enemy of Moses. Pharisaical rabbis of that age declared Him to be the destroyer of the Mosaic law and the institutes of the Torah. They proclaimed that He would bring great misfortune to the people of Israel, considering Him the violator of the holy Sabbath and destroyer of the Temple of Solomon. Therefore, they turned away from Him. Let us investigate this and discover whether such accusations were true or false. We will find that in reality Christ caused the name and prestige of Moses to become widespread. Through His efforts and teaching the Book of Moses, the Bible, became known everywhere. In fifteen hundred years there had been but one translation of the Old Testament, the Torah, which translation was made from Hebrew into Greek. But through the instrumentality of Christ's message and teachings it was translated into six hundred tongues and spread to every part of the world. All the kings and prophets of Israel were unable to promulgate the teachings of Judaism and the name of Moses beyond the borders of Palestine, whereas through Christ Judaism became an established religion in Asia, Africa, Europe and the world generally. Through the message of Christ, Moses was everywhere proclaimed a Prophet of God and His Book the Book of God. Shall we consider this Personage an enemy or a friend of Moses?

Justice is needed; we must render fair judgment upon this question. Had He been an enemy, He would not have allowed the name and teachings of Moses to become widespread in the world. He would not have promulgated the law and principles of the Torah. Would there have been any mention of Moses in America? Could even the name of Judaism have reached this part of the world through any other instrumentality? Undoubtedly, it was owing to the blessed agency and influence of Christianity that Judaism became established in this western world. Moses had no better friend and sympathizer than Christ. Consider how the illiterate among the Israelites conceal the reality of these facts and continue the delusion that Christ was an enemy of Moses. All Christians believe in Moses. They declare that He was a Man of God, the Interlocutor and Prophet of God, that His Book was the Book of God, that the people of Israel were the people of God and that all the prophets of Israel were valid and true. They offer unlimited praise, sincere eulogy, and manifest unlimited love for the religion of Moses. What harm comes from this? And if the Jews should say that Christ was also the Word of God, the Spirit of God, what harm could follow this statement? Just these few words would be the cause of reconciling the Christians and Jews. The Christians accept Moses and His Book. What harm have they suffered on account of this belief? Have they lost anything because of it?

In answer to all these questions the rabbi answered, "No."

We continued: What harm could result if the Jews were in a similar attitude toward Christianity, declaring that Christ was the Word of God, that the Gospel is the Book of God? Such an attitude as this would cause the enmity of many centuries to pass away. If we declare that Moses was the Prophet of God and that His Book was the law of God, does it harm our religious standpoint? Not at all. Furthermore, every nation is proud of its great men and heroes even though those great ones may have been atheists or agnostics. Today France glorifies Napoleon Bonaparte, saying, "He was a French military genius," whereas, in reality, he was a tyrant. They say, "Voltaire was ours," although Voltaire was an atheist. "Rousseau was a great man of this nation," and yet Rousseau was irreligious. France is proud of these great men. Feasts are held commemorating them, their names are perpetuated in special days, their memories treasured in prominent places, and there is music and celebration in their honor. The nation is proud of them. And now, do you consider these great men of France greater than Jesus of Nazareth? It is evident that in comparison with Jesus Christ they are as nothing. Consider the grandeur and majesty of Jesus in contrast with such men as we have mentioned. Consider Him from the standpoint of fame and renown. Where is the station of Christ, and where is their station? What comparison is there? In reality, Christ is incomparable. What harm, then, could come from your declaration that Jesus of Nazareth was a great man of Israelitish birth and, therefore, we love Him? That we have given to the world a great man indeed? That this mighty Personage, Whose Word has spread throughout the world, Who has conquered the East and the West, was an Israelite? Should you not be proud of Him? When you glorify and honor the memory of Christ, rest assured that the Christians will take your hands in real fellowship. All difficulty, hesitancy and restraint will vanish. Consider the troubles and persecutions heaped upon you in Russia for your fanaticism of unbelief. And you must not think that this is ended.

This humiliation will continue forever. The time may come when in Europe itself they will arise against the Jews. But your declaration that Christ was the Word of God will end all such trouble. My advice is that in order to become honorable, protected and secure among the nations of the world, in order that the Christians may love and safeguard the Israelitish people, you should be willing to announce your belief in Christ, the Word of God. This is a complete statement; there is nothing more. Is it not thoughtless, ignorant prejudice which restrains you from doing so? Declare that, verily, the Word of God was realized in Him, and all will be right.

The rabbi thoughtfully said, "I believe that what you have said is perfectly true, but I must ask one thing of you. Will you not tell the Christians to love us a little more?"

We replied, "We have advised them and will continue to do so."

15 November 1912

———————————

TALK AT HOME OF
MISS JULIET THOMPSON

———————————

48 West Tenth Street,
New York

Notes by Hooper Harris

I have spoken in the various Christian churches and in the synagogues, and in no assemblage has there been a dissenting voice. All have listened, and all have conceded that the teachings of Bahá'u'lláh are superlative in character, acknowledging that they constitute the very essence or spirit of this new age and that there is no better pathway to the attainment of its ideals. Not a single voice has been raised in objection. At most there have been some who have refused to acknowledge the mission of Bahá'u'lláh, although even these have admitted that He was a great teacher, a most powerful soul, a very great man. Some who could find no other pretext have said, "These teachings are not new; they are old and familiar; we have heard them before." Therefore, I will speak to you upon the distinctive characteristics of the manifestation of Bahá'u'lláh and prove that from every standpoint His Cause is distinguished from all others. It is distinguished by its didactic character and method of exposition, by its practical effects and application to present world conditions, but especially distinguished from the standpoint of its spread and progress.

When Bahá'u'lláh appeared in Persia, all the contemporaneous religious sects and systems rose against Him. His enemies were kings. The enemies of Christ were the Jews, the Pharisees; but the enemies of Bahá'-

u'lláh were rulers who could command armies and bring hundreds of thousands of soldiers into the arena of operation. These kings represented some fifty million people, all of whom under their influence and domination were opposed to Bahá'u'lláh. Therefore, in effect Bahá'u'lláh, singly and alone, virtually withstood fifty million enemies. Yet these great numbers, instead of being able to dominate Him, could not withstand His wonderful personality and the power and influence of His heavenly Cause. Although they were determined upon extinguishing the light in that most brilliant lantern, they were ultimately defeated and overthrown, and day by day His splendor became more radiant. They made every effort to lessen His greatness, but His prestige and renown grew in proportion to their endeavors to diminish it. Surrounded by enemies who were seeking His life, He never sought to conceal Himself, did nothing to protect Himself; on the contrary, in His spiritual might and power He was at all times visible before the faces of men, easy of access, serenely withstanding the multitudes who were opposing Him. At last His banner was upraised.

If we study historical record and review the pages of Holy Writ, we will find that none of the Prophets of the past ever spread His teachings or promulgated His Cause from a prison. But Bahá'u'lláh upheld the banner of the Cause of God while He was in a dungeon, addressing the kings of the earth from His prison cell, severely arraigning them for their oppression of their subjects and their misuse of power. The letter He sent to the Sháh of Persia under such conditions may now be read by anyone. His Epistles to the Sulṭán of Turkey, Napoleon III, Emperor of France, and to the other rulers of the world including the President of the United States are, likewise, current and available. The book containing these Epistles to the kings was published in India about thirty years ago and is known as the Súratu'l-Haykal ("Discourse of the Temple"). Whatever is recorded in these Epistles has happened. Some of the prophecies contained in them came to pass after two years; others were fulfilled after five, ten and twenty years. The most important prophecies relative to events transpiring in the Balkans are being fulfilled at the present time though written long ago. For instance, in the Epistle which Bahá'u'lláh addressed to the Sulṭán of Turkey, the war and the occurrences of the present day were foretold by Him. These events were also prophesied in the Tablet He addressed to the city of Constantinople, even to the details of happenings now being witnessed in that city.

While addressing these powerful kings and rulers He was a prisoner in a Turkish dungeon. Consider how marvelous it was for a prisoner under the eye and control of the Turks to arraign so boldly and severely the very king who was responsible for His imprisonment. What power this is! What greatness! Nowhere in history can the record of such a happening be found. In spite of the iron rule and absolute dominion of these kings, His function was to withstand them; and so constant and firm was He that He caused their banners to come down and His own standard to be upraised. For today the flags of both the Persian and the Ottoman Empires are trailing in the dust, whereas the ensign of Bahá'u'lláh is being held aloft in the world both in the East and in the West. Consider what a mighty power this is! What a decisive argument! Although a prisoner in a fortress, He paid no heed to these kings, regarded not their power of life and death, but, on the contrary, addressed them in plain and fearless language, announcing explicitly that the time would come when their sovereignty would be brought low and His own dominion be established.

He said in substance, "Erelong you will find yourselves in manifest loss. Your sovereignties will be laid waste; your empires will become a wilderness and a heap of ruins; hosts from without will invade and subdue your lands; lamentation and mourning will rise from your homes. There will be no throne; there will be no crown; there will be no palace; there will be no armies. Nay, rather, all these will be brought low; but the standard of the Cause of God will be held aloft. Then will you see that hosts and hosts will enter the Cause of God and that this mighty revelation will be spread throughout the world." Read the prophecies contained in the Súratu'l-Haykal and ponder carefully over them.

This is one of the characteristics of Bahá'u'lláh's message and teachings. Can you find events and happenings of this kind in any other prophetic dispensation? If so, in what cycle have similar things taken place? Do you find such specific prophecies and explicit statements concerning the future in the Holy Books of the past? We will now compare the teachings of Bahá'u'lláh with the Holy Words which have descended in the former cycles.

First among the great principles revealed by Him is that of the investigation of reality. The meaning is that every individual member of humankind is exhorted and commanded to set aside superstitious beliefs, traditions and blind imitation of ancestral forms in religion and investigate reality for himself. Inasmuch as the fundamental reality is one, all religions and nations of the world will become one through investigation of reality. The announcement of this principle is not found in any of the sacred Books of the past.

A second characteristic principle of the teachings of Bahá'u'lláh is that which commands recognition of the oneness of the world of humanity. Addressing all mankind, He says, "Ye are all the leaves of one tree." There are no differences or distinctions of race among you in the sight of God. Nay, rather, all are the servants of God, and all are submerged in the ocean of His oneness. Not a single soul is bereft. On the contrary, all are the recipients of the bounties of God. Every human creature has a portion of His bestowals and a share of the effulgence of His reality. God is kind to all. Mankind are His sheep, and He is their real Shepherd. No other scriptures contain such breadth and universality of statement; no other teachings proclaim this unequivocal principle of the solidarity of humanity. As regards any possible distinctions, the utmost that Bahá'u'lláh says is that conditions among men vary, that some, for instance, are defective. Therefore, such souls must be educated in order that they may be brought to the degree of perfection. Some are sick and ailing; they must be treated and cared for until they are healed. Some are asleep; they need to be awakened. Some are immature as children; they should be helped to attain maturity. But all must be loved and cherished. The child must not be disliked simply because it is a child. Nay, rather, it should be patiently educated. The sick one must not be avoided nor slighted merely because he is ailing. Nay, rather, he must be regarded with sympathy and affection and treated until he is healed. The soul that is asleep must not be looked upon with contempt but awakened and led into the light.

Bahá'u'lláh teaches that religion must be in conformity with science and reason. If belief and teaching are opposed to the analysis of reason and principles of science, they are not worthy of acceptance. This principle has not been revealed in any of the former Books of divine teaching.

Another fundamental announcement made by Bahá'u'lláh is that religion must be the source of unity and fellowship in the world. If it is productive of enmity, hatred and bigotry, the absence of religion would be preferable. This is a new principle of revelation found only in the utterances of Bahá'u'lláh.

Again, Bahá'u'lláh declares that all forms of prejudice among mankind must be abandoned and that until existing prejudices are entirely removed, the world of humanity will not and cannot attain peace, prosperity and composure. This principle cannot be found in any other sacred volume than the teachings of Bahá'u'lláh.

Another teaching is that there shall be perfect equality between men and women. Why should man create a distinction which God does not recognize? In the kingdoms below man sex exists, but the distinction between male and female is neither repressive nor restrictive. The mare, for instance, is as strong and often more speedy than the horse. Throughout the animal and vegetable kingdoms there is perfect equality between the sexes. In the kingdom of mankind this equality must likewise exist, and the one whose heart is purest, whose life and character are highest and nearest to the divine standard is most worthy and excellent in the sight of God. This is the only true and real distinction, be that one man or woman.

Bahá'u'lláh has announced the necessity for a universal language which shall serve as a means of international communication and thus remove misunderstandings and difficulties. This teaching is set forth in the Kitáb-i-Aqdas ("Most Holy Book") published fifty years ago.

He has also proclaimed the principle that all mankind shall be educated and that no illiteracy be allowed to remain. This practical remedy for the need of the world cannot be found in the text of any other sacred Books.

He teaches that it is incumbent upon all mankind to become fitted for some useful trade, craft or profession by which subsistence may be assured, and this efficiency is to be considered as an act of worship.

The teachings of Bahá'u'lláh are boundless and without end in their far-reaching benefit to mankind. The point and purpose of our statement today is that they are new and that they are not found in any of the religious Books of the past. This is in answer to the question, "What has Bahá'u'lláh brought that we have not heard before?" Therefore, it is conclusive and evident that the Manifestation of God in this day is distinguished from all former appearances and revelations by His majesty, His power and the efficacy and application of His Word.

All the Prophets of God were scorned and persecuted. Consider Moses. The people called Him a murderer. They said, "You killed a man and fled from punishment and retribution. Is it possible after your former deeds that you could become a Prophet?"

Many similar experiences are recorded concerning the holy, divine Messengers. How bitter and severe was the persecution to which They were subjected! Consider how they endeavored to efface and belittle Christ. They placed upon His head a crown of thorns and paraded Him through the streets and bazaars in mockery crying, "Peace be upon thee, thou king of the Jews!" Some would bow to Him backward, saying in scornful tones, "Thou king of the Jews!" or "Lord of lords, peace be upon thee!" Still others would spit upon His blessed countenance. In brief, the persecutions which Christ suffered during the time of His manifestation are mentioned in the books of the old cycle, Jewish, Roman or Greek. No praises were bestowed upon Him. The only recognition and acceptance offered Him was from His believers and followers. Peter, for instance, was one who praised Him; and the other disciples spoke in His behalf. Numerous books were written against Him. In the history of the Church you will find record of the hatred and antagonism manifested by the Roman, Greek and Egyptian philosophers, attributing calumnies and ascribing imperfection to Him.

But during the manifestation of Bahá'u'lláh, from the day of His appearance to the time of His departure, the people of all nations acknowledged His greatness, and even those who were His most bitter enemies have said of Him, "This man was truly great; his influence was mighty and wonderful. This personage was glorious; his power was tremendous, his speech most eloquent; but, alas, he was a misleader of the people." This was the essence of their praise, eulogy and denial. It is evident that the authors of such statements, although His enemies, were profoundly impressed by His greatness and majesty. Some of His enemies have even written poems about Him, which though intended for satire and sarcastic allusion, have in reality been praise. For instance, a certain poet opposed to His Cause has said, "Beware! Beware! lest ye approach this person, for he is possessed of such power and of such an eloquent tongue that he is a sorcerer. He charms men, he drugs them; he is a hypnotizer. Beware! Beware! lest you read his book follow his example and associate with his companions because they are the possessors of tremendous power and they are misleaders." That is to say, this poet used such characterizations, believing them to be terms of belittlement and disparagement, unaware that they were in reality praises, because a wise man, after reading such a warning, would say, "The power of this man must unquestionably be very great if even his enemies acknowledge it. Undoubtedly, such a power is heavenly in its nature." This was one of the reasons why so many were moved to investigate. The more His enemies wrote against Him, the more the people were attracted and the greater the number who came to inquire about the truth. They would say, "This is remarkable. This is a great man, and we must investigate. We must look into this cause to find out what it all means, to discover its purpose, examine its proofs and learn for ourselves what it signifies." In this way the malign and sinister statements of His enemies caused the people to become friendly and approach the Cause. In Persia the mullás went so far as to proclaim from the pulpits against the Cause of Baháʼuʼlláh casting their turbans upon the ground—a sign of great agitation—and crying out, "O people! This Baháʼuʼlláh is a sorcerer who is seeking to mesmerize you; he is alienating you from your own religion and making you his own followers. Beware! lest you read his book. Beware! lest you associate with his friends."

Baháʼuʼlláh, speaking of these very ones who were attacking and decrying Him, said, "They are My heralds; they are the ones who are proclaiming My message and spreading My Word. Pray that they may be multiplied, pray that their number may increase and that they may cry out more loudly. The more they abuse Me by their words and the greater their agitation, the more potent and mighty will be the efficacy of the Cause of God, the more luminous the light of the Word and the greater the radiance of the divine Sun. And eventually the gloomy darkness of the outer world will disappear, and the light of reality will shine until the whole earth will be effulgent with its glory."

18 November 1912

TALK AT HOME OF MR. AND MRS. FRANK K. MOXEY

---

575 Riverside Drive,
New York

Notes by Esther Foster

I offer thanks to God for this meeting with you. From the outer standpoint such meetings are inconceivable, for we are orientals whereas you are occidentals. Between us there is no patriotic, linguistic, racial, commercial nor political relation. No worldly bond nor connection of any kind exists between us that would justify such a gathering as this. The love of God has brought us together, and this is the best of means and motive. Every other bond of friendship is limited in effectiveness, but fellowship based upon the love of God is unlimited, everlasting, divine and radiant. Therefore, we must be thankful to God for uniting us in love and agreement, praise Him for creating such affinity between us that those from the faraway Orient may associate with the beloved ones of the West in the utmost fragrance.

Surely for everything there is an all-comprehending wisdom, especially for the great and important affairs of life. The supreme and most important happening in the human world is the Manifestation of God and the descent of the law of God. The holy, divine Manifestations did not reveal themselves for the purpose of founding a nation, sect or faction. They did not appear in order that a certain number might acknowledge Their Prophethood. They did not declare Their heavenly mission and message in order to lay the foundation for a religious belief. Even Christ did not become manifest that we should merely believe in Him as the Christ, follow Him and adore His mention. All these are limited in scope and requirement, whereas the reality of Christ is an unlimited essence. The infinite and unlimited Reality cannot be bounded by any limitation. Nay, rather, Christ appeared in order to illumine the world of humanity, to render the earthly world celestial, to make the human kingdom a realm of angels, to unite the hearts, to enkindle the light of love in human souls, so that such souls might become independent, attaining complete unity and fellowship, turning to God, entering into the divine Kingdom, receiving the bounties and bestowals of God and partaking of the manna from heaven. Through Christ they were intended to be baptized by the Holy Spirit, attain a new spirit and realize the everlasting life. All the holy precepts and the announcements of prophetic laws were for these various and heavenly purposes. Therefore, we offer thanks to God that although no earthly relation obtains among us, yet—praise be to God!—ideal and divine bonds blend us together. We have gathered here in this meeting, eagerly anticipating the showing forth of the divine bestowals.

In past centuries the nations of the world have imagined that the law of God demanded blind imitation of ancestral forms of belief and worship. For example, the Jews were captives of hereditary racial religious observances. The Muslims, likewise, have been held in the bondage of traditionary forms and ceremonials. The Christians also have been implicit followers of ancient tradition and hereditary teaching. At the same time the basic foundation of the religion of God, which was ever the principle of love, unity and the fellowship of humanity, has been forsaken and cast aside, each religious system holding tenaciously to imitations of ancestral forms as the supreme essential. Therefore, hatred and hostility have appeared in the world instead of the divine fruitage of unity and love. By reason of this it has been impossible for the followers of religion to meet together in fellowship and agreement. Even contact and communication have been considered contaminating, and the outcome has been a condition of complete alienation and mutual bigotry. There has been no investigation of the essential underlying basis of reality. One whose father was a Jew invariably proved to be a Jew, a Muslim was born of a Muslim, a Buddhist was a Buddhist because of the faith of his father before him, and so on. In brief, religion was a heritage descending from father to son, ancestry to posterity, without investigation of the fundamental reality; consequently, all religionists were veiled, obscured and at variance.

Praise be to God! We are living in this most radiant century wherein human perceptions have developed and investigations of real foundations characterize mankind. Individually and collectively man is proving and penetrating into the reality of outer and inner conditions. Therefore, it has come to pass that we are renouncing all that savors of blind imitation, and impartially and independently investigating truth. Let us understand what constitutes the reality of the divine religions. If a Christian sets aside traditionary forms and blind imitation of ceremonials and investigates the reality of the Gospels, he will discover that the foundation principles of the teachings of Christ were mercy, love, fellowship, benevolence, altruism, the resplendence or radiance of divine bestowals, acquisition of the breaths of the Holy Spirit and oneness with God. Furthermore, he will learn that Christ declared that the Father "maketh his sun to rise on the evil and on the good, and sendeth rain on the just and on the unjust." The meaning of this declaration is that the mercy of God encircles all mankind, that not a single individual is deprived of the mercy of God, and no soul is denied the resplendent bestowals of God. The whole human race is submerged in the sea of the mercy of the Lord, and we are all the sheep of the one divine Shepherd. Whatever shortcomings exist among us must be remedied. For example, those who are ignorant must be educated so that they may become wise; the sick must be treated until they recover; those who are immature must be trained in order to reach maturity; those asleep must be awakened. All this must be accomplished through love and not through hatred and hostility. Furthermore, Jesus Christ, referring to the prophecy of Isaiah, spoke of those who having eyes, see not, having ears, hear not, having hearts, understand not; yet they were to be healed. Therefore, it is evident that the bounties of Christ transformed the eye which was blind into a seeing one, rendered the ear which was formerly deaf, attentive, and made the hard, callous heart tender and sensitive. In other words, the meaning is that although the people possess external eyes, yet the insight, or perception, of the soul is blind; although the outer ear hears, the spiritual hearing is deaf; although they possess conscious hearts, they are without illumination; and the bounties of Christ save souls from these conditions. It is evident, then, that the manifestation of the Messiah was synonymous with universal mercy. His providence was universal, and His teachings were for all. His lights were not restricted to a few. Every Christ came to the world of mankind. Therefore, we must investigate the foundation of divine religion, discover its reality, reestablish it and spread its message throughout the world so that it may become the source of illumination and enlightenment to mankind, the spiritually dead become alive, the spiritually blind receive sight and those who are inattentive to God become awakened.

The teachings and ordinances of the divine religions are of two kinds. The first are spiritual and essential in nature—such as faith in God, faith in Christ, faith in Moses, faith in Abraham, faith in Muḥammad, the love of God and the oneness of the world of humanity. These divine principles shall be spread throughout the world. Strife and enmity shall disappear, ignorance, hatred and hostility cease and all the human race be bound together. The second kind of ordinances and teachings concern the outer conditions and transactions of the world of mankind. They are the nonessential, accidental or temporary laws of human affairs which are subject to change and transformation according to the exigencies of time and place. For instance, during the time of Moses divorce was permitted, but in the time of Christ it was made unlawful. In the Torah there are ten commandments concerning retribution for murder, which would not be possible to enforce at the present time and under existing conditions of the world. Therefore, these nonessential, temporary laws are superseded and abrogated to suit the exigencies and requirements of successive periods.

But the followers of the divine religions have turned away from the principles and ordinances which are essential and unchanging in the Word of God, forsaking those fundamental realities which have to do with the life of the human world, the eternal life—such as the love of God, faith in God, philanthropy, knowledge, spiritual perception, divine guidance—holding these to be contingent and nonessential while wrangling and disagreeing over such questions as whether divorce is lawful or unlawful, or whether this or that observance of a minor law is orthodox and true. The Jews consider divorce lawful; the Catholic Christians deem it unlawful; the outcome is discord and hostility between them. If they would investigate the one fundamental reality underlying the laws revealed by Moses and Christ, this condition of hatred and misunderstanding would be dispelled and divine unity prevail.

Christ commanded that if we are smitten upon the right cheek, we should turn the other cheek also. Consider what is happening now in the Balkans. What conformity with the teachings of Christ do we witness in that deplorable picture? Has not man absolutely forgotten and forsaken the divine command of Christ? In fact, such discord and warfare are evidences of disagreement upon the non-essential precepts and laws of religious belief. Investigation of the one fundamental reality and allegiance to the essential unchanging principles of the Word of God can alone establish unity and love in human hearts.

Throughout the Orient in the nineteenth century spiritual darkness prevailed, and the religions were submerged in the ocean of blind imitations and adherence to hereditary forms. There was no trace of the essential foundation of divine revelation. Because of this, hostility and hatred surrounded mankind; discord, rancor and warfare afflicted humanity; blood overspread the horizons of the eastern world. Instead of fellowship and agreement, religion had become the cause of hatred; instead of unity, it produced discord, enmity and strife. The conditions were similar to those existing in the Balkans today, where it might appear as if the basis of divine religion were war and conflict, the adherents of one religion seeking to extirpate and destroy another, and the adherents of both imbued with the fanatical impulse to kill. They consider the pathway to the good pleasure of God a pathway of blood, and the more a religionist kills, the nearer he draws to God. These are the results of blind imitations. How gloomy and destructive to humanity is such an outcome! If this be the foundation of divine religion, its absence is preferable; for even the infidels do not shed blood in this way, nor are they hostile toward each other. The forces of hostility and strife are the religions of the present day, and that which should have contributed to the illumination and betterment of the world has become productive of gross darkness and degradation.

To resume: Consider how similar blind imitations had made the darkness in the Orient all-encircling. At such a time Bahá'u'lláh dawned from the eastern horizon like the glory of the sun. He renewed the basis of the religions of God, destroyed blind adherence to ancestral forms and established in their stead love and spiritual fellowship so that no strife, discord or hostility remained. This reconciliation of divergent sects is visible and evident. They now live together in love and unity. If you should enter one of their meetings, you would realize that they have become as one race, one native land, one religion; that they associate together in brotherhood and agreement. Praise be to God! These blind imitations and this darkness have ceased to exist, and the reality of the oneness of humanity has been practically proven.

I consider the American people a highly civilized and intelligent nation, a nation investigating truth and reality. It is my hope that through the efforts of this noble nation the solidarity of humanity may be continually advanced, that the illumination of the human world may become widespread, that the banner of universal peace may be held aloft, the lamp of the oneness of the human world be ignited and the hearts of the

East and West be conjoined. Then the reality of the divine religions shall become resplendent and refulgent, indicating that they were meant to be the cause of unity and love and that through them heavenly bestowals have ever been conferring light upon the human world.

29 November 1912

TALK AT HOME OF MR. AND MRS. EDWARD B. KINNEY

---

780 West End Avenue,
New York

Notes by Esther Foster

This evening I wish to speak to you concerning the mystery of sacrifice. There are two kinds of sacrifice: the physical and the spiritual. The explanation made by the churches concerning this subject is, in reality, superstition. For instance, it is recorded in the Gospel that Christ said, "I am the living bread which came down from heaven: if any man eat of this bread, he shall live for ever." He also said, "This [wine] is my blood . . . which is shed for many for the remission of sins." These verses have been interpreted by the churches in such a superstitious way that it is impossible for human reason to understand or accept the explanation.

They say that Adam disobeyed the command of God and partook of the fruit of the forbidden tree, thereby committing a sin which was transmitted as a heritage to His posterity. They teach that because of Adam's sin all His descendants have, likewise, committed transgression and have become responsible through inheritance; that, consequently, all mankind deserves punishment and must make retribution; and that God sent forth His Son as a sacrifice in order that man might be forgiven and the human race delivered from the consequences of Adam's transgression.

We wish to consider these statements from the standpoint of reason. Could we conceive of the Divinity,

Who is Justice itself, inflicting punishment upon the posterity of Adam for Adam's own sin and disobedience? Even if we should see a governor, an earthly ruler punishing a son for the wrongdoing of his father, we would look upon that ruler as an unjust man. Granted the father committed a wrong, what was the wrong committed by the son? There is no connection between the two. Adam's sin was not the sin of His posterity, especially as Adam is a thousand generations back of the man today. If the father of a thousand generations committed a sin, is it just to demand that the present generation should suffer the consequences thereof?

There are other questions and evidences to be considered. Abraham was a Manifestation of God and a descendant of Adam; likewise, Ishmael, Isaac, Jeremiah and the whole line of prophets including David, Solomon and Aaron were among His posterity. Were all these holy men condemned to a realm of punishment because of a deed committed by the first father, because of a mistake said to have been made by their mutual and remotest ancestor Adam? The explanation is made that when Christ came and sacrificed Himself, all the line of holy Prophets who preceded Him became free from sin and punishment. Even a child could not justly make such an assertion. These interpretations and statements are due to a misunderstanding of the meanings of the Bible.

In order to understand the reality of sacrifice let us consider the crucifixion and death of Jesus Christ. It is true that He sacrificed Himself for our sake. What is the meaning of this? When Christ appeared, He knew that He must proclaim Himself in opposition to all the nations and peoples of the earth. He knew that mankind would arise against Him and inflict upon Him all manner of tribulations. There is no doubt that one who put forth such a claim as Christ announced would arouse the hostility of the world and be subjected to personal abuse. He realized that His blood would be shed and His body rent by violence. Notwithstanding His knowledge of what would befall Him, He arose to proclaim His message, suffered all tribulation and hardships from the people and finally offered His life as a sacrifice in order to illumine humanity—gave His blood in order to guide the world of mankind. He accepted every calamity and suffering in order to guide men to the truth. Had He desired to save His own life, and were He without wish to offer Himself in sacrifice, He would not have been able to guide a single soul. There was no doubt that His blessed blood would be shed and His body broken. Nevertheless, that Holy Soul accepted calamity and death in His love for mankind. This is one of the meanings of sacrifice.

As to the second meaning: He said, "I am the living bread which came down from heaven." It was not the body of Christ which came from heaven. His body came from the womb of Mary, but the Christly perfections descended from heaven; the reality of Christ came down from heaven. The Spirit of Christ and not the body descended from heaven. The body of Christ was but human. There could be no question that the physical body was born from the womb of Mary. But the reality of Christ, the Spirit of Christ, the perfections of Christ all came from heaven. Consequently, by saying He was the bread which came from heaven He meant that the perfections which He showed forth were divine perfections, that the blessings within Him were heavenly gifts and bestowals, that His light was the light of Reality. He said, "If any man eat of this bread, he shall live for ever." That is to say, whosoever assimilates these divine perfections which are within me will never die; whosoever has a share and partakes of these heavenly bounties I embody will find eternal life; he who takes unto himself these divine lights shall find everlasting life. How manifest the meaning is! How evident! For the soul which acquires divine perfections and seeks heavenly illumination from the teachings of Christ will undoubtedly live eternally. This is also one of the mysteries of sacrifice.

In reality, Abraham sacrificed Himself, for He brought heavenly teachings to the world and conferred heavenly food upon mankind.

As to the third meaning of sacrifice, it is this: If you plant a seed in the ground, a tree will become manifest from that seed. The seed sacrifices itself to the tree that will come from it. The seed is outwardly lost, destroyed; but the same seed which is sacrificed will be absorbed and embodied in the tree, its blossoms, fruit and branches. If the identity of that seed had not been sacrificed to the tree which became manifest from it, no branches, blossoms or fruits would have been forthcoming. Christ outwardly disappeared. His personal identity became hidden from the eyes, even as the identity of the seed disappeared; but the bounties, divine qualities and perfections of Christ became manifest in the Christian community which Christ founded through sacrificing Himself. When you look at the tree, you will realize that the perfections, blessings, properties and beauty of the seed have become manifest in the branches, twigs, blossoms and fruit; consequently, the seed has sacrificed itself to the tree. Had it not done so, the tree would not have come into existence. Christ, like unto the seed, sacrificed Himself for the tree of Christianity. Therefore, His perfections, bounties, favors, lights and graces became manifest in the Christian community, for the coming of which He sacrificed Himself.

As to the fourth significance of sacrifice: It is the principle that a reality sacrifices its own charactcristics. Man must sever himself from the influences of the world of matter, from the world of nature and its laws; for the material world is the world of corruption and death. It is the world of evil and darkness, of animalism and ferocity, bloodthirstiness, ambition and avarice, of self-worship, egotism and passion; it is the world of nature. Man must strip himself of all these imperfections, must sacrifice these tendencies which are peculiar to the outer and material world of existence.

On the other hand, man must acquire heavenly qualities and attain divine attributes. He must become the image and likeness of God. He must seek the bounty of the eternal, become the manifestor of the love of God, the light of guidance, the tree of life and the depository of the bounties of God. That is to say, man must sacrifice the qualities and attributes of the world of nature for the qualities and attributes of the world of God. For instance, consider the substance we call iron. Observe its qualities; it is solid, black, cold. These are the characteristics of iron. When the same iron absorbs heat from the fire, it sacrifices its attribute of solidity for the attribute of fluidity. It sacrifices its attribute of darkness for the attribute of light, which is a quality of the fire. It sacrifices its attribute of coldness to the quality of heat which the fire possesses so that in the iron there remains no solidity, darkness or cold. It becomes illumined and transformed, having sacrificed its qualities to the qualities and attributes of the fire.

Likewise, man, when separated and severed from the attributes of the world of nature, sacrifices the qualities and exigencies of that mortal realm and manifests the perfections of the Kingdom, just as the qualities of the iron disappeared and the qualities of the fire appeared in their place.

Every man trained through the teachings of God and illumined by the light of His guidance, who becomes a believer in God and His signs and is enkindled with the fire of the love of God, sacrifices the imperfections of nature for the sake of divine perfections. Consequently, every perfect person, every illumined, heavenly individual stands in the station of sacrifice. It is my hope that through the assistance and providence of God and through the bounties of the Kingdom of

Abhá you may be entirely severed from the imperfections of the world of nature, purified from selfish, human desires, receiving life from the Kingdom of Abhá and attaining heavenly graces. May the divine light become manifest upon your faces, the fragrances of holiness refresh your nostrils and the breath of the Holy Spirit quicken you with eternal life.

All of the talks compiled in this volume
come from *The Promulgation of Universal Peace:
Talks Delivered by 'Abdu'l-Bahá during His Visit to the
United States and Canada in 1912*
(Bahá'í Publishing Trust, 2007).

PUBLISHING

Bahá'í Publishing and the Bahá'í Faith

Bahá'í Publishing produces books based on the teachings of the Bahá'í Faith. Founded over 160 years ago, the Bahá'í Faith has spread to some 235 nations and territories and is now accepted by more than five million people. The word "Bahá'í" means "follower of Bahá'u'lláh." Bahá'u'lláh, the founder of the Bahá'í Faith, asserted that He is the Messenger of God for all of humanity in this day. The cornerstone of His teachings is the establishment of the spiritual unity of humankind, which will be achieved by personal transformation and the application of clearly identified spiritual principles. Bahá'ís also believe that there is but one religion and that all the Messengers of God— among them Abraham, Zoroaster, Moses, Krishna, Buddha, Jesus, and Muḥammad—have progressively revealed its nature. Together, the world's great religions are expressions of a single, unfolding divine plan. Human beings, not God's Messengers, are the source of religious divisions, prejudices, and hatreds.

The Bahá'í Faith is not a sect or denomination of another religion, nor is it a cult or a social movement. Rather, it is a globally recognized independent world religion founded on new books of scripture revealed by Bahá'u'lláh.

Bahá'í Publishing is an imprint of the National Spiritual Assembly of the Bahá'ís of the United States.

For more information about the Bahá'í Faith,
or to contact Bahá'ís near you,
visit http://www.bahai.us/
or call
1-800-22-UNITE

OTHER BOOKS AVAILABLE FROM BAHÁ'Í PUBLISHING

REJOICE IN MY GLADNESS
The Life of Ṭáhirih
Janet Ruhe-Schoen
$18.00 U.S. / $20.00 CAN
Trade Paper
ISBN 978-1-931847-84-1

A moving biography of one of the leading feminists of the 1800s, *Rejoice in My Gladness* traces the story of Ṭáhirih, a woman who began teaching the equality between men and women in largely Muslim Persia, and was eventually martyred for her outspokenness and courage.

Drawing on extensive research and steeped in the culture of daily life in nineteenth-century Persia, this is the definitive account of the life of Ṭáhirih—a renowned poetess and one of the leading feminists of her time. *Rejoice in My Gladness* follows the life of Ṭáhirih from her birth through her adulthood, covering important events such as her marriage, her controversial conversion to the Bábí Faith, and her execution due to her beliefs and activities. The reader will see how Ṭáhirih changed the face of women's rights forever, as she was the first woman in recorded Middle Eastern history to remove her veil before an assembly of men. At her execution, her last words have been recorded as "You can kill me as soon as you like, but you will never stop the emancipation of women."

THE QUICKENING
UNKNOWN POETRY OF ṬÁHIRIH
John S. Hatcher and Amrollah Hemmat
$18.00 U.S. / $20.00 CAN
Trade Paper
ISBN 978-1-931847-83-4

A new priceless collection of previously unpublished poems by the renowned nineteenth-century poetess, Ṭáhirih.

The Quickening is a newly translated collection of stirring poems by the renowned nineteenth-century poetess Ṭáhirih that deal with a subject that has challenged religious scholars throughout the ages. Among the world religions, no theme has attracted more attention or caused more controversy than the concept of a last judgment or end of time. The Bahá'í view of the "Resurrection," or the "Quickening," as the term is translated here, stands in bold contrast to many traditional views. It is seen as a prelude to a glorious outcome—the galvanizing of our collective will to bring about a just and lasting peace and the unification of humankind. In addition to the beautifully crafted English translation of Ṭáhirih's poems, this volume also includes her work in the original Persian and Arabic.

SPIRIT OF FAITH
The Oneness of Religion
Bahá'í Publishing
$12.00 U.S. / $14.00 CAN
Hardcover
ISBN 978-1-931847-81-0

Spirit of Faith: The Oneness of Religion is a compilation of writings and prayers that focus on the inherent oneness of all the world's great religions. Spiritual seekers of all faiths will relish these uplifting passages that underscore the unity of thought that helps us define our place within a single, unfolding, and divine creation. This collection contains writings from Bahá'u'lláh, the Báb, and 'Abdu'l-Bahá.

The *Spirit of Faith* series will explore a range of topics—such as the unity of humanity, the eternal covenant of God, the promise of world peace, and much more   by taking an in-depth look at how the writings of the Bahá'í Faith view these issues. The series is designed to encourage readers of all faiths to think about spirituality, and to take time to pray and meditate on these important topics.

COMPASSIONATE WOMAN
THE LIFE AND LEGACY OF PATRICIA LOCKE
John Kolstoe
$21.00 U.S. / $23.00 CAN
Hardcover
ISBN 978-1-931847-85-8

Compassionate Woman shares the captivating life of Patricia Locke, a Lakota Indian, who dedicated her life to righting injustices on behalf of indigenous peoples, as well as all of humanity. She was awarded the MacArthur Fellowship, was the first American Indian to serve as a senior officer on the National Spiritual Assembly of the Bahá'ís of the United States, and was posthumously inducted into the National Women's Hall of Fame.

This fascinating biography of Patricia Locke, who was given the name *Compassionate Woman*, gives us a glimpse into the life of someone dedicated to restoring justice and helping those in need. Her life of service began in Anchorage, Alaska, when she founded a community center aimed at assisting Native Americans, Eskimos, and Aleuts—who had moved to the city from villages—to cope with the many problems they encountered. She then went on to work for the Western Interstate Counsel for Higher Education, where she focused much of her energy on establishing colleges on Reservations. She was particularly concerned with improving education for American Indians, and worked hard toward advancing education on Reservations so that Native American culture and language could be woven into the curriculum. She also spent many years as a freelance writer, instructor at various universities, and activist on behalf of the poor and oppressed. In addition to the MacArthur Fellowship, Locke was the first American Indian to serve as a senior officer on the National Spiritual Assembly of the Bahá'ís of the United States, and was posthumously inducted into the National Women's Hall of Fame. Patricia Locke was wholeheartedly committed to serving the needs of others, and her indomitable spirit lives on through her legacy of service and loving compassion for all peoples of the world.